Researching with Integrity

Researching with Integrity breaks new ground by analyzing research ethics from the perspective of individual character rather than rule-based codes of practice. It challenges over-dependence on principles derived from bioethics to produce a book with relevance to a wide range of academic disciplines. Reflecting on real stories from university academics to illustrate fine-grained research dilemmas, it identifies a series of moral virtues for the modern researcher and attendant vices to be avoided. The virtues of courage, respectfulness, resoluteness, sincerity, humility, and reflexivity are closely related to ethical practice throughout different phases of research in framing questions, negotiating access, generating data and ideas, creating results, disseminating those results, and reflecting on what has been achieved. The book offers a theoretically grounded yet strongly practical approach to understanding the complexities of research ethics. As such it will be an essential resource for both serious scholars of research ethics and postgraduate students.

Bruce Macfarlane is Professor of Higher Education at the University of Portsmouth (UK) where he is also Head of Academic Development. His previous books include *Teaching with Integrity* and *The Academic Citizen*. He is a Vice Chair of the Society for Research into Higher Education.

Researching with Integrity
The Ethics of Academic Enquiry

Bruce Macfarlane

Routledge
Taylor & Francis Group

NEW YORK AND LONDON

First published 2009
by Routledge
270 Madison Ave, New York, NY 10016

Simultaneously published in the UK
by Routledge
2 Park Square, Milton Park, Abingdon, Oxon OX14 4RN

Routledge is an imprint of the Taylor & Francis Group, an informa business

© 2009 Taylor & Francis

Typeset in Minion by
Swales & Willis Ltd, Exeter, Devon
Printed and bound in the United States of America on acid-free paper by
Walsworth Publishing Company, Marceline, MO.

Library of Congress Cataloging-in-Publication Data
Macfarlane, Bruce, 1961–
   Researching with integrity : the ethics of academic enquiry / Bruce Macfarlane.
      p. cm.
   Includes bibliographical references and index.
   1. Research—Moral and ethical aspects.   2. Scholars—Professional ethics.   I. Title.
   Q180.55.M67M327 2008
   174—dc22
   2008022092

ISBN10: 0–415–42903–X (hbk)
ISBN10: 0–415–42904–8 (pbk)
ISBN10: 0–203–88696–8 (ebk)

ISBN13: 978–0–415–42903–0 (hbk)
ISBN13: 978–0–415–42904–7 (pbk)
ISBN13: 978–0–203–88696–0 (ebk)

In memory of my father
Derrick Macfarlane (1928–2005)

CONTENTS

FIGURES AND TABLES

Figures

Tables

NARRATIVES

FOREWORD

We need a new way of looking at research ethics: a way that presents ethics as a positive challenge.

Now that academic research is increasingly directed towards the needs of the wider society in a changing and complex world, its conduct is coming under increasing scrutiny. That is as it should be. But this has led to an undue focus on the negative. Regulatory frameworks, procedures, committees, guidelines and codes of practice all have their place, but they are primarily aimed at avoiding the unethical. The danger is that they encourage an attitude of mind in which jumping through the hoops in order to satisfy a committee replaces a concern for the very real ethical dimensions of enquiry. The ethical conduct of research involves more than simply the avoidance of being unethical or conforming to regulations.

In order to understand this ethical dimension we need to get behind, or beyond, the rules and regulations and the often conflicting principles they express. In practice ethical problems are often experienced in the form of a dilemma. Principles collide. Rules and regulations don't always work. As has often been said, research can be a messy business. Furthermore, ethical considerations become apparent in the mundane questions such as the order in which the authors of an article are presented as well as in the striking issues that have come to be associated, for example, with research which involves testing drugs.

It is this ethical dimension of the day-to-day work of the academic researcher that needs more attention. If academics are to research with integrity then that integrity must be a feature of the whole research process. Indeed, the researcher needs to *be* ethical.

But what are the qualities of an ethical researcher? How are academics to conduct themselves with integrity amidst the competing pressures under which they work? Bruce Macfarlane's *Researching with Integrity* provides us with a way of thinking that can enhance a positive ethical outlook. It touches upon the philosophical yet is intensely practical. Its ideas are as applicable to research in physics as in fine art.

When I finished reading the book I felt that I had been given something to help me to research in a way that expresses my values without a sense that values had been imposed upon me. In other words, this book provides a way of addressing the vital question of one's own responsibilities as a researcher.

Professor Stephen Rowland
Institute of Education and University College London
University of London

ACKNOWLEDGMENTS

I would like to thank my colleagues Neil Garrod, Jon Nixon, Roger Ottewill, Alan Skelton, John Strain, and David Watson for reading a draft of the original manuscript. Their feedback was invaluable to me and has helped me to improve the text further. I am also grateful to Stephen Rowland for writing the foreword.

The book includes a number of short narratives provided by academic researchers from a range of disciplines. While it is not appropriate to name these contributors in order to protect their privacy, I would like to acknowledge their generosity in reflecting so openly about their own experiences and uncertainties. These stories play a central role in enlivening and giving a proper context to the argument I outline.

The book has resulted from conference papers, lectures, seminars, and dialogue with academics over the last three years. This dialogue provided me with new ideas, helped me to modify some of my arguments, and enabled me to take the book in fresh directions. I was also privileged to spend three months as a Visiting Professor in the Center for Studies of Higher Education (CSHE) at Nagoya University in Japan shortly before completing the book. During this period I benefited from working with Yoshiko Saitoh. Through our conversations about research ethics in Japan and the interviews we conducted together I gained a number of important insights.

Finally, I would like to thank my wife Alice Chan for her support during the writing of this book and for proof-reading the manuscript.

INTRODUCTION
A Question of Integrity

The importance of acting "ethically" is now widely recognized as an essential element of conducting research in any context or environment. It is an injunction contained in the many books on research methods, across the sciences, the arts, and the humanities. Very few of these books exclude at least some consideration of ethics as an area of concern. Indeed, there is a plethora of titles purely devoted to the ethics of research, often focusing on the particular concerns of different disciplines.

The word "integrity" is often used in publications relating to the ethics of research. But it is a word that is more often asserted than explained. The central purpose of this book will be to identify what the word integrity means for an academic researcher regardless of their discipline. It is clear that this will have multiple meanings rather than a single or simple meaning shaped by the demands of the research process, the commitments of individuals who pursue academic investigation, their cultural context, and the circumstances they may find themselves in. My focus will be on understanding the excellences of character (or "virtues") of the researcher. Here, I will draw on the work of Aristotle and others who have written about virtue. This is a different approach to the one which is usually taken by authors of books about research ethics, who tend to concentrate on explaining how we ought to act rather than the personal qualities we ought to possess.

We tend to use the word "integrity" to invoke an ideal of human behavior. If someone is said to possess "integrity" we recognize this as a good thing but rarely set about identifying exactly what we mean by it.

Sometimes we equate integrity with qualities like honesty or trustworthiness. But it appears to mean something different according to the nature of our activities. For example, we might identify integrity in a sportsman or woman as about playing "fair" and not cheating the opposition. For a doctor it might mean protecting the privacy of patients while for a soldier it would be more likely to imply respecting the rights of non-combatants or prisoners of war. A politician with integrity might be one prepared to tell the truth or admit that a past policy position was misjudged. Hence, the meaning of integrity is a nuanced one. It depends on what activities we are engaged in.

CODES OF CONTROL

Research is, in many if not most contexts, becoming a highly regulated and closely scrutinized activity. Professional and discipline-based bodies, such as the British Medical Association and the American Psychological Association, issue guidelines or codes of practice which demand strict adherence. Failure to respect these codes carries the threat of expulsion from the profession or society. Higher education institutions have also developed their own guidelines, while ethics committees established by universities and funding bodies exercise varying degrees of power and control over the approval of research proposals. Finally, many organizations that sponsor research, such as government agencies, issue their own codes and guidelines on ethical issues connected with the research function.

For those undertaking research there is, thus, an almost bewildering mass of advice and instruction on offer. They must often satisfy injunctions regarding research ethics from their professional or disciplinary community, their educational institution, and a sponsoring organization. Invariably, codes and guidelines produced by these various parties tell researchers what they must *not* do. Largely they are aimed at controlling research activity and deterring what is perceived as "unethical" conduct. From an organizational perspective, this negative and defensive emphasis is understandable. There are quasi-legal reasons why organizations such as universities, professional bodies, or government departments need to avoid being held accountable for the actions of a rogue researcher or research team. Damage to an organization may extend beyond reputation to financial loss where legal action succeeds. Commonly, researchers are implored to avoid harming their research subjects, mainly psychologically in the case of human beings or physically in the case of animals. They are also called on not to breach the confidentiality of their relationship with a research subject so that the views of an individual can be kept anonymous in subsequent reporting of research findings. At the same time, in medical research, there is often a concern that the costs of undertaking research in terms of the possible pain and suffering caused to human subjects and animals should be outweighed by the potential longer-term benefit to society through identifying a procedure or treatment for alleviating a particular condition.

Education and training offered to researchers in universities, colleges, and other educational settings tends to reflect this ethical agenda. It is an agenda dominated by a concern for the rights of (mainly) human subjects and the costs and benefits of undertaking research. Sets of principles are written down to which researchers are expected to adhere. These principles emphasise how important it is not to be unethical and frequently consist of little more than an explanation of an operating code of conduct. Contradictions between principles are left unexplained and unexplored. Once granted permission to proceed, few regulatory committees or panels take an interest in the ethical dilemmas researchers might face. They act as gatekeepers to the research process rather than ethical mentors or guides.

REAL RESEARCH ETHICS

What I believe is lacking in the approach to research ethics found in much of the literature, codes of practice, and university training is how to positively encourage ethical conduct. Developing an understanding of what to do is always a more challenging prospect than issuing edicts about what is not right. This demands that any discussion about research ethics is located in the complex and ambiguous context in which it takes place. This is a context populated by individuals and groups with differing personal goals, ambitions, and ideological perspectives. "Real" research is about the stuff of human life: hope and disappointment, loyalty and betrayal, triumph and tragedy. This is one reason why following a code of ethics is likely to be of limited help when confronted with ethical issues whilst actually *doing* research.

Another problem is that codes of research ethics tend to deal with a very limited range of ethical issues, implicitly defining the word "research" in rather narrow terms. For example, codes tend to say a lot about dealing with research subjects and the treatment of data but very little about relationships between researchers (who often work in teams) or between researchers and their sponsors or institutional employers. Nor do they engage with the researcher as an individual in terms of the trials and temptations that will almost inevitably lie ahead.

For example, the success of academic careers is normally determined by converting research into publication "outputs" such as journal papers or books. A fine line divides creative presentation of results and exaggeration or fabrication (Grinnell, 2002).

By their nature, codes of research ethics tend to enunciate certain core principles such as "confidentiality," "informed consent," or "respect for persons." Inevitably, though, the search for truth through research will sometimes bring some of these principles into conflict. Classically, a number of researchers have argued that "undercover" methods which deliberately ignore issues of informed consent are justifiable on the basis of the benefit society gains from learning the truth. In some cases, it is also argued that deception is the only effective means of researching the cultural practices of certain groups in society, such as football hooligans or nightclub bouncers (Calvey, 2000).

There are other ways in which it is artificial to neatly divide the world of "research" and "research ethics" from other roles performed by those who conduct research. Many academic staff in universities and colleges are "research-active," in the sense of researching and publishing in their specialist field, while, simultaneously, performing teaching and management duties. These other roles can make significant demands on their time and cannot be divorced from the organizational culture in which individuals work. Academic departments, and the universities in which they operate, behave on the basis of very different disciplinary cultures. Their research practice is shaped by these cultural differences. Research-oriented staff are likely to face conflicting demands, for example, in universities (and departments) which depend largely on income from teaching activities. Further, the imperative to "do" research is a strong motivational force for many academics, regardless of the formal support for such activity which institutions may offer (Knight, 2002). This can create tensions within academic departments and potential role conflicts.

FOCUSING ON CHARACTER

In short, codes of practice offer little assistance to those looking to cope effectively with the ethical demands of research activity. What is needed is an alternative approach to the education and development of academic staff undertaking a research role. This is something that this book sets out to develop. The approach will be based on a view of ethics that seeks to empower rather than restrict discussion of key issues by focusing on the character, or "virtues," of the researcher. Short stories or "narratives" will be used to form a vehicle for discussion of ethical issues in research. These are examples of ethical concerns or crises that real researchers have experienced in conducting an investigation. These narratives will be presented in relation to different stages or phases of the research process: *framing* (or reframing) research questions; *negotiating* with affected parties; *gathering* data or other materials; *creating* new theories, methods, critiques, and other forms of knowledge or practice; *disseminating* the results or findings of investigation; and finally, *reflecting* on the research process itself.

Narratives will be drawn from both novice and experienced researchers in a range of disciplines across the arts, humanities, natural, social, and applied sciences including accountancy, archaeology, chemistry, economics, education, environmental science, history, law, management, mathematics, and social work. They represent problems connected with a host of dilemmas: sharing academic credit for research, determining the extent to which one can trust the research findings of others, issues connected with confidentiality and consent, representation of the purpose of research to research subjects, power relations between researchers and research subjects, and exercising patience when collecting data. Narratives are used because they are an appropriate means of illustrating the types of real, live situations which researchers face "in the field." Discussion of these scenarios, gathered over the last three years, will be informed by the views of researchers working in higher education.

The narratives help to illuminate a set of virtues and vices that may be mainly associated with each stage or phase of the research process. The virtues which I identify—*courage, respectfulness, resoluteness, sincerity, humility,* and *reflexivity*—represent some (but not necessarily all) of the excellences of character needed to be a "good" researcher. They form an illustrative rather than exhaustive list and are intended as a means to explore a virtue-based approach to understanding research ethics rather than a prescriptive formula. At the same time, it is hoped that they will resonate with the reader regardless of whether they are an inexperienced or more seasoned researcher. The extent to which these narratives are seen to have relevance across academic disciplines will also determine how successful I have been in fixing upon particular virtues. They are intended as the mean point between extremes of behavior or "vices." Each virtue will be presented with two connected vices at opposite ends of a behavioral scale. Sliding away from the virtue at the mid-point of this scale is all too easy. It is only by recognizing these parameters to each virtue that we are able to make sense of the mid-point or virtue and what it means to act "with integrity."

EDUCATING FOR INTEGRITY

In writing this book, I hope that it will prove of use both to those who practice research and those who teach research ethics, often as part of some formal education or training programme. The narratives are in themselves materials that may facilitate a discussion of real-life research, enabling examples from practice to foreground any more theoretical understanding of ethical dimensions. My ideas on how a virtue approach might be implemented in the classroom are contained in the last section of the book together with an evaluation of the impact of an increasingly performative culture on the ethics of research.

Finally, this book represents the completion of a personal project seeking to map the nature of academic practice from a virtue ethics perspective. My ideas on the ethics of teaching in higher education and the academic service role may be found in two of my previous books, *Teaching with Integrity* (Macfarlane, 2004) and *The Academic Citizen* (Macfarlane, 2007a). My hope is that this book, along with the others, will make some modest contribution in re-balancing our understanding of what it means to be a modern academic through a revised appraisal of the ethical dimension.

PART ONE

FROM PRINCIPLES TO VIRTUE

1

THE LEGACY OF NUREMBERG

The "betrayal of Hippocrates" had a broad basis within the German medical profession. (Ernst, 2001, 42)

INTRODUCTION

The phrase "research ethics" conjures up a set of concerns which is now largely taken for granted. It invokes a language, and a related set of questions, that mainly clusters around the treatment of research subjects. Are we treating such people with dignity and ensuring that their rights are fully respected? Is any data collected kept confidential? Is the anonymity of the research subject respected? In biomedical research this implies a duty not to harm someone who has agreed to participate in a study. In all forms of research involving humans one might ask whether there is "informed" consent. In other words, does the research subject *really* understand what they are letting themselves in for?

These are just some of the crucial questions in any consideration of research ethics but, as I will argue in subsequent chapters, not the only relevant ones to ask. If we are to understand the ethical challenges of research it is important to consider not just the duty of the researcher toward the research subject but the development of character necessary to navigate through the temptations of the entire research process.

This chapter will be concerned with the roots of research ethics. Why is research ethics today virtually synonymous with the treatment of research subjects? The answer to this question can be found largely through examining the lessons learned from the history of medical research during the twentieth century. I will focus on two notorious chapters from this history to illustrate their profound effect on our contemporary understanding of research ethics and reflect on the ethical theories that underpin the dominant principles which have emerged in response to this legacy.

THE NAZIS AT NUREMBERG

On June 2, 1948, seven Nazi doctors were hung at Landsberg prison in Bavaria. Among those sent to the gallows that day was Professor Karl Gebhardt, chief surgeon to the SS who held the rank of Major General and President of the German Red Cross. He was one of 20 medical doctors who had been tried before the International Military Tribunal at Nuremberg accused of war crimes. At the so-called "Doctors' Trial," Gebhardt was found guilty, *inter alia*, of performing medical experiments, without the consent of the subjects, on both prisoners of war and civilians of occupied countries, thereby taking part in the mass-murder of concentration camp inmates. He had co-ordinated surgical experimentation, mainly on young Polish women, at concentration camps in Ravensbrück and Auschwitz. Here, Gebhardt oversaw operations where victims were deliberately inflicted with battlefield wounds as a means of pursuing his interest in reconstructive surgery. Many were to die or suffer intense agony and serious injury as a result of Gebhardt's operations.

The atrocious crimes committed by Nazi doctors like Gebhardt, or more infamous counterparts such as Josef Mengele, need to be understood as more than the actions of a few "mad" or "bad" men. The doctors found guilty at Nuremberg were the tip of a much bigger iceberg of complicity and wrong-doing within the German medical profession. Several hundred doctors were captured and tried at the end of the war by the Soviets, like Carl Clauberg, a professor of gynecology who conducted X-ray sterilization experiments on Jewish and Roma women without the use of anaesthetics. Many others, probably the vast majority, escaped punishment altogether. According to one estimate, around 350 doctors behaved in a criminal manner (Mitscherlich & Mielke 1949). Underlying this statistic, however, is a broader-based "betrayal of Hippocrates" within the German medical profession (Ernst, 2001).

The focus of the Nazi regime of the 1930s on military and race-based policies meant that scientists and medical academics were central to the pursuit of the political agenda. The pre-war Nazi regime introduced a number of measures, including legalized forced sterilization of disabled people and involuntary euthanasia for those deemed "unworthy of living" such as children with Down's syndrome. These policies meant that doctors played a prominent executive role in Nazi society as "experts" on decision-making juries. A much higher percentage of doctors joined the Nazi party and its associated organizations, than comparable professions (Ernst, 2001). This is an oft-quoted indicator of the complicity of large swathes of the medical profession with Nazi policies. The actions of Gebhardt and his associates had a profound effect on the lives (and deaths) of tens of thousands of victims and their families. These actions also had a highly significant long-term effect on the development of research ethics in medical science and, as we will see, on other disciplines too.

The lack of clear international ethical standards for the conduct of scientific research was one of the excuses put forward on behalf of the defendants at the Doctors' Trial. It was true that no formal code was in operation at this time but the "Hippocratic oath" had been, from the fourth century BC, the commonly accepted moral basis on which doctors were governed. Attributed to the Greek physician Hippocrates, this "oath" has a number of ancient and modern interpretations but, in essence, is based on the central tenets of treating patients with respect and to the best of one's ability. However, while no international ethical code may have existed at the time of the Doctors' Trial, the standards against which they were judged were *ex post facto* norms that any civilized human being should have understood (Jonsen, 1998). In other words, the lack of an international code was considered no excuse by the tribunal for treating human beings purely as a means to an end, and without humanity.

Another excuse put forward by the Nazi doctors was that some of the prisoners on whom they experimented had already been sentenced to death. Hence, it was argued that their experiments made no material difference to their fate; these prisoners would die anyway. In a clear repudiation of this excuse and the abhorrent actions of the defendants, the judgment in the Doctors' Trial included what is now known as the "Nuremberg Code." This was a 10-point statement of ethical and moral principles that, according to the court, should underpin medical research and experimentation in the future (see figure 1.1). At the heart of the Nuremberg Code is the principle of "voluntary consent." This established that respectful treatment of human subjects must be the central tenet of any "ethical" research.

The publicity afforded to the Nuremberg Trials means that public attention has tended subsequently to focus on Nazi doctors as those most closely associated with cruel and unethical experimentation on human subjects. However, while they may have received comparatively less subsequent scrutiny, during World War II many similar abuses were carried out by the Japanese imperial army involving allied prisoners of

---

A summary of the principles:

* Voluntary consent of the human subject is essential.
* The research subject may withdraw consent at any time.
* The results should be for the good of society.
* The risk should not exceed the humanitarian benefit.
* All safety precautions must be taken.
* The research design should be justified and based on expertise.
* The investigator must be scientifically qualified.
* The experiment must be terminated where the subject's health is threatened.

Based on Katz (1972).

Figure 1.1 The Nuremberg Code (1949).

war (McNeill, 1993; Powell, 2006). It is estimated that several thousand Chinese and Russian prisoners died during human experiments to develop chemical and biological weapons, particularly in Japanese-occupied Manchuria. In one of the most notorious incidents of abuse during this period most of the members of the crew of an American B-29 bomber were captured after crash landing in Japan. Eight members of the crew were taken to a university medical department in Fukuoka where they died after vivisection operations in which most of their vital organs were removed. Biological warfare experiments were also carried out by the Japanese in at least 11 Chinese cities during its period of occupation (McNeill, 1993).

The lessons learnt from these war time abuses meant that the principles contained in the Nuremberg Code shaped the development of subsequent post-war international accords on ethics such as the Declaration of Helsinki adopted in 1964 by the World Medical Assembly. It would be naïve, however, to think that the principles contained in the Nuremberg Code and the lessons learned from Nazi treatment of concentration camp victims have led to the elimination of unethical behavior in medical research.

While the Nuremberg Code represents a profound statement of moral principles shaped by the horrors of Nazi experimentation the modern-day regulation of scientific research owes more, in reality, to a scandal that broke in the USA in 1972.

THE TUSKEGEE SCANDAL

On May 16, 1996 President Bill Clinton issued a formal apology to the remaining survivors and victims of a 40-year medical research experiment, the longest non-therapeutic human experiment in the history of public health. The experiment set out to study the long-term effects of syphilis, a blood-related bacteria that can be contracted through sexual contact or inherited from a mother. President Clinton's apology was designed, at least in part, to re-establish the trust and confidence of African Americans in medical research. After the scandal broke in 1972, the study, entitled the "Tuskegee Study of Untreated Syphilis in the Negro Male," became synonymous with the exploitation of African Americans. Tuskegee was not a scientific research study that simply went wrong. It was a methodical, longitudinal study that exposed a deep-seated and long-term disregard for the well-being of research subjects exploited on the basis of their race and class (Reverby, 2000).

The origins of the study go back to the early 1930s when the U.S. Public Health Service at Tuskegee Institute invited black males from a poor and racially segregated area of Alabama for a free medical examination. The real purpose of these examinations was to select around 400 men to take part in a longitudinal study into the effects of syphilis. On the basis of these examinations, men with suspected syphilis were invited back for further tests and spinal taps as a means of tracking the progress of the disease. The men in the trial were told that they were being treated for "bad blood" and were given incentives to attend for continuing "treatment" such as free burial insurance and hot meals.

At the time that the study began the only known treatments for syphilis were mercury or salvarsan. Mercury was largely ineffectual and dangerous (Cornwell, 2006). Effective treatments only emerged following the discovery of penicillin and the development of antibiotics after World War II. However, the syphilitic men of Tuskegee were not treated with either salvarsan or antibiotics despite the fact that the study continued until 1972 when effective treatments had been widely available for several decades. Their poverty and ignorance was systematically exploited and, worse, the men were denied proper treatment for a condition that led, for some, to an early and painful death. By the time that the study was halted it is estimated that up to 100 men had died. Later, the U.S. government paid about $10 million in out of court damages, equivalent to £37,500 per participant (Cornwell, 2006).

Other post-war scandals demonstrated the need for regulation and oversight of biomedical research activity. The testing of an experimental drug known as thalidomide was another high-profile example. Thalidomide was designed to prevent nausea and vomiting in pregnant women but tragically resulted in thousands of babies being born without limbs or with other deformities. Worse still, the drug company tested thalidomide on women without their consent or the knowledge that they were taking part in a drug trial. The scandal resulted in the Kefauver-Harris Bill, which became law in 1962. The Act created the Federal Drug Administration and led to greater testing of new medical products. The legislation also required that companies gain the consent of patients before using them as research subjects.

Tuskegee was perhaps the most influential scandal in the regulation of research ethics. The case was a chilling reminder that the cruel and exploitative treatment of research subjects did not end with the Nazis and the adoption of the Nuremberg Code. Tuskegee was instrumental in leading to federal legislation in the USA in 1974 that also established a National Commission for the Protection of Human Subjects of Biomedical and Behavioral Research. The commission was charged with the task of identifying the basic ethical principles that should underlie the conduct of biomedical and behavioral research involving human subjects and in developing guidelines which should be followed to ensure that such research is conducted in accordance with those principles.

DOMINANT ETHICAL PRINCIPLES

In 1979 the U.S. National Commission produced what became known as the Belmont Report (National Commission for the Protection of Human Subjects in Biomedical and Behavioral Research 1979). This identified three key principles for the ethical conduct of research: respect for persons, beneficence, and justice. The first of these principles meant that researchers should treat participants as autonomous agents with the right to be kept fully informed of the process. They should ensure that persons with diminished autonomy, such as children or adults without full mental capacity, are protected. The principle of beneficence implies that the benefits of participation should outweigh any harm to participants. Justice means that the selection of subjects should be fair and those who are asked to participate in research should also benefit from it. Among the ethicists who advised the Commission were Tom Beauchamp and Jim Childress from the Kennedy Institute of Bioethics at Georgetown, University of Washington. In the same year as the report, they published what has subsequently become a highly influential text on bioethics and research ethics more generally (Beauchamp & Childress, 1979). While Belmont had identified three principles, Beauchamp and Childress came up with four: autonomy (in place of respect for persons), beneficence (to act for the benefit of others), non-maleficence (the duty to do no harm), and justice.

> • Respect for persons
>   ○ subjects should be treated as autonomous agents and be fully informed
>   ○ persons with diminished autonomy should be protected
> • Beneficence
>   ○ benefits of participation should outweigh any harm
> • Justice
>   ○ selection of subjects should be fair and those who are asked to bear the burden should also benefit
>
> National Commission for the Protection of Human Subjects in Biomedical and Behavioral Research (1979).

Figure 1.2 The Belmont Report Principles (1979).

The four principles identified by Beauchamp and Childress have become collectively known as "principalism" or the "Georgetown mantra." The mantra draws on a mix of ethical theories and influences that have their roots in the philosophical writings of Immanuel Kant, the utilitarians, and John Rawls. In explaining the basis of these principles it is necessary to briefly explore the way that moral philosophy has influenced their construction.

Respect for Persons

The first of the principles, "respect for persons," derives from Kant's (1964) categorical imperative. Kant was a German philosopher who sought to demonstrate the role of reason as the basis of human morality. His categorical imperative states that human beings should act only according to rules that they would be willing to see everyone follow. Kant regarded this principle as an appeal to logic. It begs the simple question: what if everyone did that? Unless someone is prepared to see their own actions "universalized" it makes no logical sense to carry them out. As one would not wish to be treated disrespectfully merely as a means to an end this implies that we should not treat other people in a relevantly similar way. This is referred to as the "reversibility" argument: how, in other words, would you feel if someone did that to you? Kant's categorical imperative makes intuitive sense in relation to thinking about the treatment of research subjects. Through reversibility, it demands that we place ourselves in their position. Would you be happy to be treated in this way if you, as the researcher, were in the position of the research subject? If the answer is yes, this provides a moral guide to the rightness of the action. If the answer is negative, then one should desist in treating the research subjects in this manner. The use of Kantian logic is attractive especially if researchers have themselves been research subjects making them, perhaps, more emotionally equipped to empathize with the position of those they are researching.

Kant insisted on the "rational" nature of his theory. However, critics have pointed out that applying the tests of universability and reversibility does not preclude acts of "bad morality" (Bennett, 1994). This phrase refers to acts based on an individual's own sense of morality which may, nonetheless, be based on principles that many others might disapprove of. A Nazi who fervently believes that all Jews should be exterminated may, if asked to place him or herself in their position, still believe it is rational and right to carry out potentially fatal medical experiments on such research subjects. Bennett (1994) argues that the "bad morality" of Heinrich Himmler, the leader of the SS during World War II with overall responsibility for the Nazi concentration camps, was based on a set of principles. However odious, by sticking to these principles, Himmler felt his course of action was right. While this may be an extreme example, it serves to illustrate the point that the categorical imperative cannot legislate for cases of "bad morality" where we might disagree with the appropriateness of universalizing an action.

Beneficence (and Non-Maleficence)

The second principle found in the Belmont Report is that of beneficence. This principle requires that someone acts in a way that benefits others, such as a doctor seeking to benefit their patient through a course of treatment. In prescribing a drug, for example, a doctor will need to make a balanced judgment about the potential harm it might do, such as the risk of known side-effects, as opposed to its benefits as an effective treatment for a particular condition. In applying the principle of beneficence it is almost impossible to do this in isolation from its corollary, non-maleficence, or the duty to do no harm, adopted by Beauchamp and Childress as their fourth principle. This may be illustrated by reference to vaccinations. These can benefit most people and society as a whole by reducing the incidence of major diseases but there is often a small risk that some individuals may suffer some side-effects. In a broader context, public policy-makers will be concerned about the financial cost of any treatment. Can the public system of health care afford to pay for expensive, specialist treatments? Can this be justified in terms of human benefit or "happiness"?

The principle of beneficence, and much of public policy-making in health care treatment, has its roots in the theory of utilitarianism. This asserts that the utility or sum of happiness resulting from an action should be greater than the harm or disutility it causes. Unlike Kantianism which focuses on *duty* as a basis for determining the right course of action, utilitarianism is about *consequences*. Essentially, utilitarianism is concerned to ensure that the result of a moral act produces the most utility (to maximize happiness or minimize misery) for *all* persons affected by an action. In debates about research experiments using animals a simple "act" utilitarian position is frequently invoked by supporters of vivisection who contend that the harm caused (to animals) is less than the (potential) benefits derived for human good in terms of finding cures for a variety of diseases and conditions. A utilitarian calculus may also provide justification for overriding the wishes of an individual with regard to their own health or well-being. The principle of beneficence places doctors in a difficult position where the "good" of a patient might be felt to justify a degree of paternalism, such as treating a teenager with an eating disorder or an elderly patient with dementia where the consent of the individual can be difficult to establish.

There are many conventional criticisms of utilitarianism, a full analysis of which falls outside the scope of this book. However, in brief, utilitarianism is concerned with a consequentialist calculation rather than considering how we, as the actor in a decision, may feel about a particular situation (Williams, 1994). It also begs complex questions about how we define and, indeed, calculate "happiness" and leads to arguments with regard to which pleasures are worth more than others. Of particular relevance to research ethics, arguments surround the way that simple utilitarianism appears to discount the happiness quantum of animals as opposed to humans in debates about vivisection. Another difficulty is that utilitarianism appears to reject any notion of absolute human rights (Finnis, 1994). Where the availability of medical treatments is restricted in relation to the age of a patient, this can be an example of calculating the "happiness" of people in terms of perceptions of their quality of life. It may also take the form of prioritizing the interests of those deemed to have more potential quality of life, such as putting resources into the treatment of young children rather than the elderly.

Act utilitarianism justifies any action assuming it maximizes human happiness, even killing a fellow human being (Williams, 1994). It might be argued that some rules, such as not to kill a fellow human being, are in the interests of everyone since were simple utilitarianism logic to be applied to any and every situation we might all, potentially, be at risk (of being killed). If this were the case, we would all suffer greater unhappiness through fearing for our own personal safety. A Hobbesian "state of nature" without the protection afforded to citizens through a set of rules would be in no one's interests. Hence, rule utilitarianism is based on identifying rules that, when followed, maximize happiness. Laws governing human society may be understood through the prism of this logic. There are, though, circumstances where to kill may be justified, such as in self-defense. Here, a rule exception would be allowed. While there are complex theoretical arguments surrounding rule utilitarianism the important point to note is that this moral philosophy has been influential in shaping the way society is governed. General rules we need to follow as researchers that are considered to maximize happiness and minimize harm are derived from rule utilitarianism. Hence, for different motives, both Kantianism and rule utilitarianism may determine that mistreating research subjects is inappropriate. For the Kantian, this would be based on the duty not to mistreat a fellow human being while for the rule utilitarian this would be because such a rule is essential to maximize utility.

Justice

The third principle identified in the Belmont Report is justice. There are several forms of justice. Distributive justice is not so much concerned with individual acts as with the morally correct distribution of wealth, power, property, and obligations between individuals in society. The notion of justice as "fairness" adopted in the Belmont Report owes much to the work of John Rawls (1971). Rawls argued that social and economic inequalities can only be tolerated if they produce the greatest benefit to the most disadvantaged members of society. People are born into radically different social and economic circumstances. The relative prosperity of one's country of birth and family situation means that nobody is born equal. However, Rawls asks us to imagine what we would wish for if we were to be born without foreknowledge of such circumstances but were aware of the various, unequal, possibilities. In this "veil of ignorance," the rational response to not knowing, according to Rawls, is to opt to enter a society in which those with the very worst chances in life would be treated as favorably as possible. Rawls' concept of "justice as fairness" has similarities to Kant's categorical imperative since he asks us to make a rational choice based on a reversible logic.

In relation to the Belmont Report, justice was chosen as a principle to guide the fair selection of research subjects and to ensure that those selected to bear this "burden," in reference to medical experimentation, ought also to benefit. If cancer sufferers take part in trials for a new drug for the treatment of their condition they ought to be among the first to receive the full benefits of using this drug if the trial proves a success and the drug is subsequently approved for use. This is only just.

Rawls' theory of distributive justice has important implications for researchers who are working to exploit the commercial benefits of new discoveries and medical treatments. Arguably, applying Rawls' veil of ignorance test, such discoveries and treatments should be affordable and available to the least advantaged members of society rather than just those who can afford to pay for them. Patents are normally designed to protect commercial interests and produce a monopoly that raises the price of medicine although occasionally the intention of the applicant is to guard against commercial exploitation where they wish to gift an invention for the benefit of society. Rawls' analysis is also especially pertinent in a developing world context where it is important to try to view things from the perspective of the local population (Olweny, 2007). Here, researchers from the developed world working in collaboration with Western pharmaceutical companies can be accused of exploitative behavior when they benefit from the local knowledge of aboriginal people to develop new patented medicines (see chapter 4).

CONCLUSION

This chapter has mainly focused on biomedical research both in relation to the historical mistreatment of research subjects and the subsequent development of "principalism." While biomedicine may represent only a small sub-set of academic disciplines in which research of some form is conducted it has been disproportionately influential in shaping our contemporary cross-disciplinary understanding of what is meant by "research ethics." Beauchamp and Childress's four principles, closely allied to the Belmont Report, predominate in the teaching of research ethics today (see chapter 11) and, as will be demonstrated in the next chapter, through codes of research ethics adopted by research organizations including universities. While the vital importance of respect for persons has been demonstrated in this chapter by examining notorious abuses of human rights in research, there are problems inherent in seeking to transfer a set of principles derived from a consideration of bioethics into other academic disciplines.

2

CHALLENGING PRINCIPLES

Conformity to a code of ethics is no guarantor of ethical practice.
(Hughes, 2005, 231)

INTRODUCTION

The Doctors' Trial at Nuremberg and the Tuskegee syphilis scandal demonstrated that not all scientists are committed to basic standards of ethical behavior. The resulting loss of trust has led to the increasing regulation of scientific research. This system of control is based, in large part, on the principles developed by bioethicists in the wake of Tuskegee. These principles have become synonymous with ethical conduct in research. Their influence has thus spread across many academic disciplines well beyond the medical and biosciences from which they were derived. They have been formally adopted in the codes of ethical conduct of a wide range of organizations concerned with research including universities, professional bodies, public and private funding bodies, and other government agencies.

This chapter will illustrate the extent to which the Georgetown mantra has spread in practice mainly in relation to university regulations. More fundamentally, the chapter will question whether these principles provide the right basis for understanding the ethical challenges of research. Do they promote the engagement of researchers with ethical debate and personal responsibility or do they represent a facet of organizational risk management? It is the contention of this chapter, and indeed this book, that such principles fail to provide an adequate analysis of the ethical challenges of research in practice or engage researchers in a meaningful discussion about moral choices.

ETHICS CREEP

The history of research ethics is peppered with high-profile scandals that have highlighted serious shortcomings in the behavior of scientists and other researchers, normally in relation to the treatment of human subjects. The scope of this book precludes a detailed examination of these incidents. What is pertinent, however, is that the "moral panics" that have followed exposure of research scandals, such as Tuskegee, have led to the development of codified principles associated with research ethics.

Many of the most publicized of these scandals have centered on biomedical research where misconduct has led to the abuse and death of research subjects. While the ethical aspects of other fields of academic study, such as business or law, are also scrutinized, the ethics of the research process itself has tended to be of more interest to those working in the biomedical sciences. This has resulted in the emergence of "bioethics" as a sub-discipline in its own right devoted to understanding the ethical implications of biological research. Bioethicists, such as Beauchamp and Childress, have been instrumental in shaping our modern-day understanding of what is meant by research ethics. Their book, *The Principles of Biomedical Ethics*, is now in its fifth edition and is widely used in undergraduate and postgraduate ethics programs aimed at medical students and researchers. Bioethicists have become a growing academic community through which the ideas of Beauchamp and Childress have been debated, disseminated, and popularized. In a UK context, their text, and the four principles of biomedical ethics which it contains, has become practically an article of faith in the training of general practitioners (Gardiner, 2003). The Beauchamp and Childress principles have informed almost all subsequent initiatives in the development of ethical codes, including the Council for Science and Technology universal ethical code for scientists proposed by the UK government's chief scientist, Sir David King.

Since 1991, local research ethics committees have been established in the UK National Health Service (NHS) to review proposed research on NHS patients. The emergence of such committees may be partly explained by the migration of nursing and midwifery training into the university system during the 1990s and increased research activity among health professionals. It has also been given an added impetus by more recent scandals that have revealed a lack of respect for the dignity of human subjects or their remains. In the late 1990s it came to light that both Bristol Royal Infirmary and the Royal Liverpool Children's Hospital at Alder Hey had been involved in retaining the hearts of dead children, without the full knowledge or permission of parents. While a subsequent report into the Alder Hey scandal held an infant pathologist to blame, it also criticized the University of Liverpool for under-funding his professorial position and failing to supervise or monitor his work properly. A subsequent UK government report recommended that universities needed to do more to monitor the work of medical researchers employed jointly with health bodies.

Elsewhere in the world, high-profile scandals have also been the precursor for the introduction of formal codes of research ethics into the university system. One of the key drivers for the development of research ethics in Japan has been a number of well-publicized cases of scientific fraud which occurred in 2006 (Rovner, 2007). A University of Tokyo investigation into the published work of a biochemistry professor concluded that he had failed to accurately record research data. A similar case at Osaka University led a school ethics committee to conclude that a bioscience professor had falsified research data against the wishes of co-authors. Finally, a chemistry professor at Waseda University was found to have misappropriated research funds.

In response the Japanese Ministry of Education produced its own set of basic principles concerning research misconduct. The document requires Japanese universities to adopt their own regulations and respond appropriately to allegations of wrong-doing (MEXT, 2006). Shortly after the Ministry guidelines were issued, the Science Council of Japan (SCJ) produced a much-awaited code of conduct which is intended to apply to academics working across all academic research fields (SCJ, 2006). As well as outlining eight ethical principles the code refers to "the recent spate of misconduct by scientists taking place in Japan" (SCJ, 2006, 1) and the dangers this poses for the integrity of science. This is a reference to the damage that research misconduct can do to public trust in academic work (see chapters 7 and 10).

Universities and other organizations that commission research are increasingly aware and concerned about the possible damage, both financially and to reputation, of "unethical" research. Professional bodies, such as the American Psychological Association, have developed their own codes of practice, heavily influenced by the principles contained in the Belmont Report. At the forefront of this "ethics creep" are research ethics boards or committees who are interpreting their remit in an increasingly strict and narrow way in determining what is "ethical" research (Haggerty, 2004). While there is a moral argument for closely monitoring research activity there is also a strong legal one. From this perspective, a university could be held liable if it permits an academic which it employs to conduct research without putting in place checks to ensure that these activities do not breach certain basic ethical principles, such as respect for human subjects. A legal action by someone who feels that they have been harmed by the research in some way, either physically or emotionally, could result in the employing organization being held vicariously liable for any wrong-doing.

While most attention has focused on the teaching relationship, the possibilities of legal action also surround the research role of academics, especially where students are used as research subjects. It is increasingly apparent that the legal relationship between universities and their students is a contract for the provision of services (Davis, 2001). In 2007, the Canadian Supreme Court awarded substantial damages to a distance learning student for the actions of one of their professors in negligently misinterpreting part of an assignment as an admission of sexual abuse (Palfreyman, 2007). The extension of the law of negligence to include "academic malpractice" is still in its infancy (Palfreyman, 2007). However, it means that the activities of researchers are now regarded by university authorities and administrators as a "risk" that needs to be managed.

ETHICAL CLEANSING

The extent of the influence of principalism may be demonstrated through an analysis of the codes of practice and attendant guidance on research ethics by leading research councils, universities, and popular textbooks concerned with "research ethics." Each year government-backed research councils in the UK alone are responsible for allocating £1.3 billion in grants and a further £800 million in supporting research institutes and international facilities. There are eight publicly funded research councils in the UK. They place a responsibility on universities as "the research organization" to ensure that research conducted by academics employed by them is scrutinized in relation to "ethical issues" before it begins.

> The Research Organization is responsible for ensuring that ethical issues relating to the research project are identified and brought to the attention of the relevant approval or regulatory body. Approval to undertake the research must be granted before any work requiring approval begins. Ethical issues should be interpreted broadly and may encompass, among other things, relevant codes of practice, the involvement of human participants, tissue or data in research, the use of animals, research that may result in damage to the environment and the use of sensitive economic,

social or personal data. (Biotechnology and Biological Sciences Research Council, 2007, 33)

An identical statement may be found in guidelines issued by the Arts and Humanities Research Council (AHRC) and both research bodies follow relevantly similar statements to those issued by the Medical Research Council (MRC) and the Economic and Social Research Council (ESRC). The adoption of this statement by the AHRC is notable in that research in the arts, and the conceptualization of ethical issues, can be quite distinct in form and content from the human, natural, and social sciences. Indeed, until recently the use of formal scrutiny processes was unusual in the arts and humanities as well as the physical and engineering sciences (Hazlehurst, 2004). This may partly be explained by reference to the fact that research in the arts often excludes the use of animals or human subjects. Moreover, in the arts and humanities, research is often small-scale, and not always empirical nor externally funded. Despite this fact, the influence of principalism is such that the largest institution for the teaching of art and design in the UK, the University of the Arts, has adopted the Georgetown mantra of "beneficence and non-maleficence" as the two central principles in its code of practice on research ethics (University of the Arts, 2007).

It is now a standard requirement that academics wishing to undertake any form of research which involves human subjects in any way must seek "ethical approval" from a university research ethics committee or board. In the United States, such a requirement has been in place since the early 1980s while in Canada similar conditions have applied since 1998 (Grayson & Myles, 2005). The requirement is now common in the UK and increasingly may be found elsewhere in the world, such as South Africa (Louw & Delport, 2006). In a UK context, a typical example of the impact of such requirements is reported in a paper by an arts researcher, Jenny Hughes (Hughes, 2005). In the paper, she reflects on her experiences of seeking approval from her university's research ethics committee to undertake a project exploring the relationship between performance and war, externally funded by the former UK Arts and Humanities Research Board. All student and faculty researchers at Hughes' institution are required to seek ethical approval from a research ethics committee, established by the University Senate, if their work involves human subjects.

Jenny Hughes' research area is concerned with applied theatre, blending arts, history, and culture. As such she found the nature of the language used in the guidelines for seeking ethical approval alien. These guidelines were premised on the discourse of medical and experimental scientific research. For example, the committee wanted to know whether the researcher would undertake any "invasive procedures" and referred to research "subjects." In this respect, they are not untypical of the approval guidelines found at any other university but reflect an in-built bias toward the concerns and language of medical and other forms of scientific research. Criticism of approval processes though is not confined to researchers working in the arts. Medical scientists have also spoken out about the excessively time-consuming, cumbersome, and bureaucratic procedures associated with the standardization of such applications. Here, it is argued that the administrative burden has become disproportionate to the risks entailed in the vast majority of research (Jamrozik, 2004).

As a researcher in the arts, Jenny Hughes describes the process of seeking ethical approval as unsatisfactory in a number of ways beyond the use of language associated with the medical sciences. Her project involved collecting data in a war-torn country. She reflects that by carrying out research in a war zone, there were, subsequently, a number of incidents "in the field" that put the researchers at physical risk (as opposed to the research subjects). She regards the process of applying for ethical approval as essentially a distraction from the "real" ethical issues she faced as a researcher.

> Ethical practice is an ongoing interaction of values in shifting contexts and relationships rather than something delivered by a signed consent form or adherence to a static set of principles. (Hughes, 2005, 231)

What this researcher raises is that real research (and research ethics) is a "lived" experience and not one which can be neatly captured in an ethical approval form. It is also a lived experience shaped by different disciplinary cultures and methods of investigation. This goes beyond any sense of divide between science and the arts or between quantitative and qualitative research. Research involves changing contexts, evolving relationships and, above all, unanticipated consequences: things that simply happen and require the researcher to be adaptable to these circumstances.

Satisfying the requirements of ethical approval may equally hinder or damage the effectiveness of quantitative survey research. In sending out questionnaires to collect data from human subjects it is normal practice to provide a covering letter explaining the nature of the research and assuring potential respondents about the confidentiality of the process. However, an overly legalistic and defensive interpretation of the duty to ensure participants understand such rights by a research ethics board, often through issuing a detailed consent form, can have deleterious consequences. Receiving "an unfriendly letter laden with ethically correct jargon" (Grayson & Myles, 2005, 295) can make potential respondents suspicious of the research and, thus, less likely to respond to a questionnaire. In a Canadian context, Grayson and Myles (2005) argue that the "unreasonable demands" (p293) of research ethics boards have caused a drop in response rates in social sciences research. A poor response rate has knock-on effects on the quality of any piece of research, the most serious of which is that the sample is less likely to reflect the typical characteristics of the group or population being studied. Tests for statistical significance are less likely to be meaningful, making it harder to confirm or disconfirm a hypothesis. Sending out reminders or seeking further participants in a study as a result of a poor response rate will also add to the financial cost of the research.

PROBLEMATIC PRINCIPLES

The practical impact of the dominance of principalism is that research ethics is now defined largely in terms of issues connected with the treatment of human subjects. Those seeking to comply with these requirements must ensure informed consent, the avoidance of deception, the right of research subjects to withdraw, debriefing participants on the outcomes of research, and the maintenance of confidentiality. The dominance of this agenda is reflected within text books concerned with research ethics aimed at postgraduate students and new researchers. Homan (1991) recognizes this agenda in the following terms:

> (there is) a "common core" in all professional codes of research ethics . . . access to subjects, the acquisition and informing of consent, rights of subjects such as privacy and confidentiality, precautions to be taken in the interests of the reputation of the profession, obligations to colleagues and sponsors and care to be taken in reporting, speaking and publishing. (Homan, 1991, 19)

Homan's book is typical in devoting chapters to "codes and control," "privacy," "informed consent," "covert methods," "writing and publishing," and "effects" on a range of groups affected by the research including subjects. Even the chapter on writing and publishing is concerned with confidentiality and anonymity. The issue of "truth" is covered in just under two pages in a book of approximately 200 pages.

The dominance of the principles to which Homan refers may be illustrated by identifying the most commonly occurring key words and phrases in the codes of research ethics issued by leading research funding organizations and universities. These are an expression of the implications of the Georgetown mantra (see figure 2.1).

An example of the way in which these principles are reflected in a UK university code of practice on research ethics is contained in figure 2.2. This incorporates a series of statements which reflect a university's expectations regarding the conduct of research involving human subjects, based upon widely accepted principles and practices. Key words or phrases are italicized.

While the principles contained in figure 2.1 and 2.2 contain important considerations for anyone undertaking research, they also present at least two significant theoretical shortcomings.

Respect for others/autonomy
Informed consent
Confidentiality
Anonymity
Voluntary participation
Beneficence
Non-maleficence/avoidance of harm
Justice
Balancing risk and benefit
Integrity

Figure 2.1 Dominant Principles in Codes of Research Ethics.

- Minimal *risk* of harm to participants and researchers
- Potential for *benefit* by society
- Maintenance of the *dignity of participants*
- Minimal *risk* of harm to the environment
- Voluntary *informed consent* by participants, or special safeguards where this is not possible
- *Transparency* in declaring funding sources
- *Confidentiality* of information supplied by research participants and anonymity of respondents
- Acknowledgment of assistance
- Appropriate publication and dissemination of research results
- Independence and *impartiality* of researchers

University of Greenwich (2007).

Figure 2.2 General Principles Informing a University Research Ethics Policy.

Conflicting Mix of Ethical Theories

The first of the problems with principalism is that it incorporates an eclectic mix of deontology and utilitarianism. "Respect for persons" is a principle that draws on the work of Kant. According to Kant's categorical imperative, treating people with respect is a logical act since no one would wish to be treated as a means to an end. The practical effect of this principle should be that no one is exploited as part of a research project. Yet, the principle of beneficence is premised on act utilitarianism, an ethical theory that focuses on seeking to maximize utility (or happiness). This means that an act may be "ethical" in utilitarian terms if the consequences justify it. In practical terms, this would permit someone to be used as a means to an end if the benefits for mankind or utility made it justifiable in utilitarian terms. Individual rights are "trumped" by the assumed benefit which would be derived on the basis of a particular action (such as a piece of research) by a larger number of individuals.

When applied to specific situations, the eclectic mix of principles derived from the Belmont Report can be perceived as nebulous and confusing (Fisher & Kuther, 1997). This is mainly because the first order principles of Kantianism and utilitarianism conflict. In the University of Greenwich ethics policy (see figure 2.2) there is an emphasis both on protecting the rights of individuals and, at the same time, seeking to evaluate the risks and benefits of research for society. Three of the principles relate closely to a Kantian perspective by emphasizing the dignity of the individual and ensuring confidentiality, while a further three are essentially about deploying a utilitarian calculus via an assessment of risks and benefits.

A good example of where Kantianism and utilitarianism can clash is in respect to obtaining informed consent from research subjects. This refers to ensuring that the research subject understands the full implications of participating in a piece of research, with an awareness of both the risks and the benefits. A Kantian perspective would insist on the primacy of ensuring that individuals are fully aware that they are being used as research subjects with the right to withdraw this consent at any time. To do otherwise would be exploitative of individual goodwill, something that would not be a rational rule if universalized. There may, though, be situations where, from a utilitarian perspective, the research might be considered as "justified" on the basis of the potential benefits it promises to bring for society as a whole. Most research subjects are able to give their "informed" consent but there are some for whom this is arguably very difficult, especially those in a dependent power relationship to the researcher, such as students of lecturers, or those suffering some form of mental impairment. An example might be research on patients with Alzheimer's disease, a progressive loss of brain function affecting over 700,000 people in the UK alone.

The Rational Decision-Maker

While principalism lends a strong focus on the treatment of research subjects, it casts the researcher in the role of an impartial arbiter when faced by a moral dilemma. However, researchers are moral agents who must make decisions based on the vagaries of particular situations. In reality, can such decision-making be "objectified" and cast as a deductive, rational process? Making such decisions involves engaging with a set of complex feelings and motives that the three principles of Belmont or the four offered by Beauchamp and Childress are unlikely to sufficiently represent. They allow little room for the personal beliefs or values of moral actors to enter the fray. Proponents of principalism tend to characterize emotional responses to moral scenarios in a negative rather than a positive way. Yet, society tends to distrust individuals who fail to show emotion, such as those suffering from psychopathic personality disorders (Gardiner, 2003). It is dangerous to ask people to "strip away" their emotional reactions when making decisions about moral issues.

The influence of principalism has also shaped codes of research ethics that reflect the assumptions and shortcomings of these principles. They tend to emphasize the conventional "God's eye view" of research positions, representing the researcher as a detached and "scientific" observer removed from the phenomenon they are exploring (Harraway, 1988). Those committed to phenomenographic forms of research would contend that the researcher cannot be separated from the research process in this way. Similarly, some ethicists would contend that research ethics cannot, and should not, be neatly separated from the personality and beliefs of the researcher.

The Focus on Individual Human Subjects

A further difficulty with codes of research ethics is that their strong focus on the treatment of human subjects, while central to the ethical conduct of research, tends to overshadow a range of other ethical challenges that face researchers. This is reflected in the emphasis of codes of conduct and university research ethics committees on satisfying a "front-ended" agenda concerning issues such as permission, access, confidentiality, and informed consent. This characterizes the ethics of research as little more than a set of quasi-legal restrictions prior to undertaking empirical work. Here, there is a real danger that researchers will disengage with research ethics, treating applications for proceeding with a piece of research as a paper exercise involving a metaphorical "jumping through hoops." In reality, researchers are faced by a complicated range of ethical decisions and dilemmas throughout the research process and in disseminating their results and ideas. This is not restricted to gaining permission to proceed but includes all the decisions, and temptations, that researchers face in the process of developing their intellectual work and sharing it with others.

Principalism places a strong emphasis on respecting the rights of the *individual* research subject. Here, it is important to acknowledge that these principles have been shaped largely by Western philosophical thought with its stress on individualism rather than collectivism. By contrast, in Asian and Japanese culture the needs of the group are often elevated above those of the individual. Status and rank play a critical role derived from Confucianism, a moral tradition that is deeply ingrained in Japanese society (Luhmer, 1990). Hence, researchers from such a cultural context may interpret their obligations somewhat differently despite the importation of Western bioethical principles into Asian countries such as Japan (Akabayashi & Slingsby, 2003) (see chapter 5).

Context and Practice

Finally, the principles embraced in most codes are based on an understanding of research issues from the perspective of the natural and biological sciences rather than the social sciences, the arts, and the humanities. Research in these latter areas tends to depend far less upon the use of human subjects or animals than in the "hard" sciences. In the humanities, such as history, a researcher might be more concerned with the critical interpretation of sources while in arts subjects the focus of investigation might be on creative experimentation with forms and content (Brew, 2001a). This means that the types of ethical issues faced by a researcher in, say, the fine arts is likely to be different in nature to those encountered by, for example, a biochemist.

Codes of research ethics normally state their commitment to principalism but then remain silent about the complexity of putting these principles into practice. Firstly, there is the difficulty of which principle should have priority when two or more clash. Guidance on such conflicts is usually absent and this means that they are of limited use in dealing with real research issues in the field. The fine-grained nature of many issues in research ethics can be unanticipated and here codes can give the false impression that they are comprehensive documents. In reality, they provide very little assistance.

The difficulty of applying principles in practice brings us back to the depersonalized nature of principalism. No account is taken of the character and personality of the researcher who is, in effect, discouraged from engaging with their own feelings and beliefs in favor of a more "rational" approach based on balancing a set of contradictory principles.

CONCLUSION

Codes of research ethics may reflect good intentions. However, they are also artificial constructs that reflect the key tension at the heart of research ethics. One set of principles relate to respecting the rights and autonomy of the individual. However, researchers are also implored to balance the risks and benefits of conducting any investigation. Imploring researchers to do both is a standard expectation but one which is of limited value in informing real decision-making. This requires an explicit engagement with someone's own values or moral norms. Principalism tends to encourage an understanding of research ethics that can be uncoupled from character. Perhaps inadvertently, the dominance of principalism means that it is easier for researchers to hide behind a set of excuses based on intellectual justifications rather than on personal moral choices.

No code of ethics can operate without being interpreted by the individual through their own value system. Practice can often depend on making fine-grained individual choices which represent the "least bad" course of action rather than any ideal. Here, we have to depend on the integrity of the individual, which means that to really understand research ethics we need to engage with our own *character* and belief system.

3

DEVELOPING INTEGRITY

The best research will satisfy the dictates of *integrity*, moral and intellectual. (Gregory, 2003, 78)

INTRODUCTION

Nestling among the principles to be found within many codes of research ethics is the term "integrity." While this word is sometimes used as a synonym for honesty it is often used to imply something more far-reaching. Yet, the broader meaning of this word is rarely explained or explored in relation to research ethics. Worse still is the prevalence of deficit-style or negative definitions of "integrity" carried in codes of research ethics. Here, there is a tendency to concentrate on what is meant by a *lack* of integrity or, in other words, misconduct such as the falsification of data or plagiarism. The shorthand is "FF&P" which stands for fabrication, falsification, and plagiarism (Judson, 2004). The focus is on "bad" behavior rather than what we mean by being a "good" researcher.

This book is concerned with developing a positive definition of what it means to research "with integrity." The purpose of this chapter is to outline the basis of such an approach drawing on "virtue" theory. This refers to the identification of virtues or excellences of character that are associated with living a "good" life. It is an approach that contrasts sharply with the dominance of the principles discussed in the last chapter. Here, the analysis will draw on the nature of character as a guide to ethics rather than providing prescriptive rules or principles as a basis for action.

THE POSSIBILITIES OF VIRTUE

What does it mean to be "good"? This is a question which has concerned philosophers since the dawn of time. One way of attempting to answer this question is to start by identifying the things we admire about people who, in the language of today, might be referred to as "role models." These "good" people tend to possess certain admirable qualities or character traits such as honesty or loyalty. This is the basis of virtue theory: identifying excellences of character rather than relying on de-personalized principles as a moral guide.

Based on the work of Aristotle, and also found in Confucian and Christian writing, virtue theory was out of fashion for a long period before being revived by contemporary theorists such as Anscombe and MacIntyre (Anscombe, 1958; MacIntyre, 1981). A virtue is a "trait of character, manifested in habitual action, that is good for a person to have" (Rachels, 1999, 178). Virtues represent median positions between extremes of behavior, otherwise known as vices. An example of a virtue might be courage. In a war a soldier might be expected to act with courage in fighting an enemy. Running away from a battle due to a lack of courage would be classified as cowardice while, at the opposite extreme, excessive aggression might result in recklessness unnecessarily endangering the lives of compatriots. Hence, courage really represents a median position between the extremes (or vices) of cowardice and recklessness (see chapter 4).

For the purposes of this book, virtue theory offers an alternative basis for understanding the moral challenges of research. Unlike applications of rule-based theories like utilitarianism or Kantianism, virtue theory does not prescribe a course of action given a particular set of circumstances but expects people to strive to be true to the excellences of character which are widely acknowledged to form the basis of being a good person. A good person, it might be hoped, will be more likely to do the right thing in a challenging set of circumstances, such as those faced regularly by researchers. The absence of rules in virtue theory means that individuals must take personal responsibility for decisions rather than justifying actions on the basis of a de-personalized but rational rule or principle for making a judgment. Virtue theory may appear old fashioned and "moralistic" but it has had a profound impact on the development of contemporary sets of professional values. In this respect, virtue theory offers a way of understanding research ethics that breaks with the limitations of principalism.

While some virtues may appear timeless, in reality they come in and out of fashion according to the changing norms of society. A good example of this is the virtue of stoicism. Derived from the stoics who belonged to a philosophic school founded by Zeno, a stoical person is one who manages to control his or her emotions. This may involve putting up with hardship or pain without complaint. Among other things, being "stoical" can involve controlling the urge to cry when unhappy or in pain. In a British context, being stoical when faced by emotional challenges used to be thought of as a virtue. However, there is evidence that it is being rapidly displaced by an expectation that people will adopt a disposition of greater (emotional) openness. A much quoted example of this changing norm is the criticism levelled at the Queen following the death of Diana, Princess of Wales in 1997. The Queen's public control of her emotions was interpreted negatively by some people as a display of emotional coldness. In a previous era, her public reserve would have been interpreted more positively, rather than negatively, as stoicism in the face of adversity. There are, of course, significant cultural differences in respect to the extent to which one might expect to see the (public) display of emotion, such as at a funeral. In some Western countries a failure to control emotion might be frowned upon as a sign of a weakness of character, while in other cultures crying would be expected as demonstrating in front of others that the mourners cared for the person who has died. Indeed, in some cultures it is common to hire wailers to attend a funeral.

This example demonstrates two important things: virtues can vary across cultural contexts and are themselves subject to changing societal mores. They can, in other words, be contingent on the social and historical context. MacIntyre (1966) points out that Aristotle's own list of moral virtues contained several which were principally about the manners expected in "polite society" (p68) at the time he was writing connected with the expectations of "gentlemanly" behavior. However, it would be a mistake to think that this means there is no common core of virtues which can traverse cultural contexts. The "gentlemanly" virtues of Aristotle's Greek society which were linked to one's social status in society at the time may be distinguished from virtues that cross the bounds of time and different cultures such as courage, restraint, or agreeableness (MacIntyre, 1966). Virtues are central to any civil society.

Hence, certain virtues, such as honesty or loyalty, are not unique to a "Western" or "Eastern" culture. This does not mean, though, that they are necessarily interpreted in exactly the same way. In Asian cultures respectfulness may be interpreted differently than in Western society, moderated by a greater emphasis on the collective rather than the individual (see chapter 5). Virtues also straddle secular philosophy and religious traditions (Alderman 1997). Moreover, virtues that appear in the work of Aristotle, such as justice, may be found in the history of Christian thought, while benevolence, sincerity, filial piety, and right-eousness are central to Confucian teaching (Fengyan, 2004). These examples indicate how a virtue-based approach to ethics resonates far and wide.

INTELLECTUAL AND MORAL VIRTUES

The rest of this chapter will concentrate on how virtue theory might be applied to the study of research ethics forming a framework for the second part of the book. A starting point in this respect is provided by Aristotle's distinction between intellectual and moral virtues. While the exact nature of this distinction has been open to a variety of interpret-ations, intellectual virtues are normally characterized as stemming from the intellect whereas moral virtues are related to the soul. Intel-lectual virtues are about possessing cognitive faculties, such as vision or memory, which make it possible to discover the truth (Greco, 2002). By contrast, moral virtues are about good habits or dispositions to do the right or "proper" thing. Emotion or passion comes into play more with respect to moral virtues and they are shaped by custom rather than rationality.

Aristotle identified a number of moral virtues including courage, truthfulness, friendliness, justice, and (proper) pride (Aristotle, 1906). "Proper" pride is about having self-respect rather than a boastful self-regard for one's own importance. He also cited five intellectual virtues. The theoretical, intellectual virtues consist of philosophical wisdom (*sophia*), scientific or empirical knowledge (*episteme*), and intuitive understanding (*nous*). In addition to these three is the virtue of prac-tical wisdom or prudence (*phronesis*) and the productive virtues of art, skill, and craft knowledge (*techne*). Later, St Thomas Aquinas div-ided intellectual virtue into two categories: speculative ones concerned with seeking understanding, wisdom, and scientific knowledge, and practical ones connected with prudence and the arts. For Aquinas, while moral virtues help us determine what we want to achieve, the intellectual virtues are vital in helping us achieve these ends. Hence, his four "cardinal" virtues consist of three moral virtues—justice, temperance and fortitude. These are characteristics of a "good" man. However, men also need prudence, a final intellectual virtue, in order to exercise the faculty of wisdom that makes it possible to achieve the other three (Gilson, 1929).

Applying the distinction between moral and intellectual virtues to the research environment, intellectual virtues might consist of dispositions such as curiosity, creativity, intellectual rigor, and judgment (or *phrone-sis*). A researcher must be sufficiently interested to pursue the answer to a research question or project in the first place (curiosity), be able to create something original such as a new model, design, or critique (creativity), be capable of adopting a questioning approach to existing knowledge and practices (intellectual rigor), and have the *nous* (or judgment) to decide such things as what to include or omit from a study and which results are significant and which are not. We make intellectual judgments based on our knowledge and skill but make moral judgments based on our sense of what is right or wrong in human relations.

THE RESEARCH PROCESS

Moral virtues need to be lived out at all stages when "doing research." There are, though, many different ways of conceptualizing the research process just as there are different ways of defining the word "research" (Vermunt, 2005). The meaning of research may be interpreted as information gathering, discovering the truth, insightful exploration and discovery, analytic and systematic enquiry, incompleteness, re-examining existing knowledge, a problem-based activity, or, even, a set of misconceptions (Meyer et al., 2005). This demonstrates that there is no uniform understanding of the meaning of research although there are common strands connected with the notion of testing out the truth and going on an intellectual journey of discovery.

The metaphor of research as "a journey" is a common way of understanding the research process (Brew, 2001b). It implies a continuous process of discovery leading, in some cases, to personal transformation. The journey is something which involves a long-term, possibly career-spanning commitment. In addition to the journey metaphor, Brew (2001b) identifies three further conceptions of the research process. The "domino" conception interprets research as a more atomistic process. Here, separate elements are linked together synthesizing different structural components in a linear form. By following this process questions are answered or problems get solved. Research may also be explained according to a "layer" conception. This involves "discovering, uncovering or creating underlying meanings" (Brew, 2001b, 280). Brew links this conception more closely with research as an artistic process involving creativity rather than discovery. Finally, Brew identifies a fourth conception which she labels as "trading." This emphasizes research as a social phenomenon and the money, prestige, and recognition with which it is associated. Publications, grants, and social networks hold the key to trading in this social market place.

Literature and poetry have been a source of inspiration for a number of other writers who have sought to explore different conceptions of research. Comparing the investigatory styles of characters from fictional detective novels has been recommended as a way of demystifying research methodology (Thorpe & Moscarola, 1991). The theoretical, rational approach of Agatha Christie's Hercule Poirot is contrasted with the scientific method of Sherlock Holmes or the more intuitive style of a detective who likes to go "undercover," such as Maigret. Delamont (2005) draws on James Elroy Flecker's poem, *The Gates of Damascus* as an extended metaphor for exploring and explaining the directions a researcher may take. Flecker's poem describes four gates by which the traveller can leave the safe city of Damascus. The Aleppo Gate is for trade and commerce. This draws parallels with contract research where sponsors are looking for solutions to policy problems. While this type of research may be necessary in forging an academic career it may also require researchers to make sacrifices in terms of pursuing their own epistemological or intellectual agenda. The Mecca Gate is for pilgrims devoted to a particular faith. This route is indicative of work where the researcher stays within his or her methodological or ideological paradigm. By contrast, the Baghdad Gate and the Lebanon Gate are more challenging and dangerous exits. Travelling through these gates increases the risk of loneliness, depression, and failure but, ultimately, the intellectual rewards are potentially much greater (see chapter 6).

RESEARCH PHASES

A somewhat less abstruse way of conceptualizing the research process is by reference to different stages or phases. This has parallels with Brew's (2001b) domino conception. Initially, a researcher normally needs to frame the nature of their research question, problem, or issue at hand. This means thinking through what it is they want to research and often designing some kind of proposal for a project or study. Here, the boundaries of the study need to be made clear, by laying out what will and will not be within the scope of the research. A researcher must then enter into negotiations to gain access to organizations and communities, gain the consent of participants, and obtain the necessary permission to proceed. The third step may be characterized as the gathering phase and involves, depending on the discipline, the collection of data, materials, ideas, and, perhaps, sources of inspiration. The researcher must then move on to analyzing and evaluating what he or she has gathered. This stage involves the creation of results, models, designs, concepts, and artefacts. It is a "creative" stage as it calls on the researcher to convert their "raw" data into results or give meaning to or an interpretation of a set of materials. These creative products of the research process must then be disseminated. Here, the researcher will publish, exhibit, or perform their work. Finally, the researcher might usefully spend time reflecting on the extent to which they have succeeded in pushing back the boundaries of knowledge and learnt personally from the process. This reflective process enables them to decide in which direction to take their future research work. These phases are summarized in table 3.1 and provide a starting point for applying virtue theory to the research process.

Similar interpretations of stages within the research process may be found in a wide range of books and national reports. For example, a report on occupational standards for researchers identified six stages in the research process: gathering information from secondary sources, preparing research briefs, developing research designs, carrying out investigations, analyzing data, and recording research and findings (Geary et al., 1997). While this model does not contain an emphasis on developing research questions, dissemination, and reflection, it presents essentially a domino conception.

There is a dynamic, rather than necessarily linear, relationship between the research phases I have outlined. For example, while reflection might occur at the end of a research project it could arise as an ongoing consideration for more reflective individuals. Dissemination might take the form of reporting and discussing one's methodology rather than the results of research which may be gathered at a later stage. Equally, while dissemination ought to occur before the end of a project, some researchers will start this process considerably earlier

Table 3.1
Research Phases

Phase	Meaning
Framing	questions, problems, hypotheses, issues, projects, proposals
Negotiating	access, consent, permission, time, support
Generating	data, materials, ideas, inspiration
Creating	results, interpretations, models, concepts, theories, critiques, designs, artefacts
Disseminating	through publication, exhibition, performance
Reflecting	on epistemological and personal learning

than others and feed this into their process of reflection and, potentially, the redrafting of research questions. Moreover, research questions or problems might need to be reframed during the research process if the gathering or creating phase proves disappointing or unproductive. This may even require a return to negotiating access to a different set of interviewees. It may mean reconstructing a questionnaire or another element of the research design. "Negotiating" will not necessarily be the second step in the research process where a researcher has established ongoing access to individuals or organizations from a previous investigation. For more seasoned researchers, reflecting on their last piece of research may be a more natural starting point in generating fresh ideas or a new research design. This is particularly pertinent given the increasing maturity of "first time" researchers undertaking doctoral and other postgraduate research degrees, many of whom are mid-career professionals (Gordon, 2005; Leonard et al., 2005).

Table 3.1 seeks to provide a general framework for understanding the processes that underpin research spanning the academic disciplines. While it is intended to be inclusive there is a need to apply the framework with sensitivity to different discipline-based research cultures. Geographers gather information "in the field" while a researcher in English may spend more time working in a library. A researcher in physics, on the other hand, may look to explore and discover something new in the laboratory using tools and machinery (Robertson & Blackler, 2006). The way that research is "framed" can be quite different according to the methodological disposition of the investigator. Some will frame formal hypotheses and test out this proposition deductively while others will develop more open-ended questions and look to explore through inductive methods. The "dissemination" of results in the arts often takes a different form than that prevalent in the natural, human, or social sciences where publication through books, reports, or academic journals is the norm. This includes "hearing it, viewing it, reading it or experiencing it in other ways" (Strand, 1998, 54). Thus, exhibitions and creative performances are forms of dissemination for research in the arts. How research takes place and where it is disseminated may vary across the disciplines but the key phases are essentially comparable.

The starting point for researchers may be related to their professional experience which could include research activities or relevant participant observations. Some readers may, therefore, find it more helpful to think of the research phases as a "cycle" providing a more flexible starting point (see figure 3.1). For human, natural, and some social scientists such a cycle may involve the identification of more formal

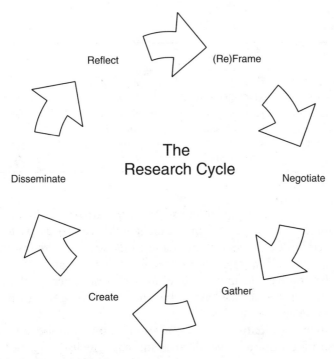

Figure 3.1 The Research Cycle.

hypotheses and experimental stages. Artists may also be able to relate their research to a developmental cycle involving the generation of ideas, selecting materials, and then designing, constructing, and revising them through to final production (Collinson, 2005).

VIRTUES AND VICES

While a conception of research as a series of phases, or as a cycle, has its limitations, it is principally intended as a heuristic device for discussing the impact of the virtues and vices beyond conventional discussion of research ethics in relation to approval procedures and the treatment of human subjects. These different stages present particular demands on researchers and give rise to expectations that they will demonstrate a series of moral virtues and steer clear of certain corresponding vices. This set of virtues and vices represent the ideal character of the researcher and the temptations they face during what is a demanding social and intellectual process (see table 3.2).

Detailed discussion of the virtues and vices presented in table 3.2 will form the core of this book. They will often be related to the real-life

Table 3.2
The Virtues and Vices of Research

Phase	Vice (deficit)	Virtue	Vice (excess)
Framing	Cowardice	*Courage*	Recklessness
Negotiating	Manipulativeness	*Respectfulness*	Partiality
Generating	Laziness	*Resoluteness*	Inflexibility
Creating	Concealment	*Sincerity*	Exaggeration
Disseminating	Boastfulness	*Humility*	Timidity
Reflecting	Dogmatism	*Reflexivity*	Indecisiveness

narratives of ethical issues obtained from researchers from a number of disciplines. They will be presented and discussed as part of the second section of this book and serve to illustrate the moral expectations that individual researchers have of themselves and others. They reveal the motives, feelings, and desires of researchers and indicate when researchers feel they have either met or fallen short of their own values and expectations.

The virtues I identify draw inspiration from a number of sources aside from the work of Aristotle and Aquinas. The list of virtues draws on the work of others in conceiving of the possible interplay of virtue in the research process. Pring (2001) identified the importance of dispositions such as courage, honesty, modesty, and humility in connection with being an educational researcher although, I believe, such virtues have a resonance and relevance well beyond a single academic discipline. Nixon (2004) contends that truthfulness, respect, and authenticity are pivotal in framing the nature of academic life as a whole. Others working from a more avowedly research perspective have identified characteristics of a "good" researcher which are, in effect, virtues. For example, perseverance, bravery, honesty, and a willingness to take criticism are among the personal qualities that research supervisors believe characterize "good" researchers (Kiley & Mullins, 2005).

It is important to recognize that virtues are ideal dispositions and, as such, any one individual is unlikely to possess them all. Here, the personality of the researcher comes into play. Virtues may be grouped according to different character traits such as empathy, order, resourcefulness, and serenity (Cawley et al., 2000). Possessing empathy, for example, consists of sub-traits including concern, consideration, and sensitivity. People's personalities differ. This means that, in the case of researchers, some may be more empathetic or sensitive in their treatment of research subjects than others because this is a particular strength associated with their personality. Similarly, Pincoffs (1986) identifies instrumental and non-instrumental virtues. Instrumental virtues are associated with getting things done, such as persistence in enquiry, whilst non-instrumental virtues, such as respectfulness or sensitivity, are not action oriented in the same way. Some people are more disposed towards instrumental virtues than others. In terms of the virtues identified in relation to research (see table 3.2), respectfulness is clearly a less action-oriented or instrumental virtue than, say, resoluteness.

There are also said to be gender-based differences between the way men and women resolve moral problems. Here, it is claimed that the adolescent male will deploy a rights approach in resolving dilemmas while young women will exercise a "care" approach based on giving a higher priority to the importance of relationships (Gilligan et al., 1988). Differences between men and women have been linked to different stages of moral development. Kohlberg's well-known six stage model of universal moral reasoning includes two stages which are said to reflect male and female dispositions (Kohlberg, 1984). According to Jaffe and Hyde (2000), stage 3 of this model, focused on the maintenance of relationships and meeting the expectations of others, is most commonly associated with the behavior of women. By contrast, stage 4, which relates to compliance with the law to maintain the social order, is modal among men. Hence, it is important to be realistic. Everyone is different and few researchers will possess all the ideal dispositions. Recognizing what they might be, and where an individual may have strengths and weaknesses, though, seems a sensible starting point.

EXPLORING "INTEGRITY"

Any list of virtues is contentious. Why, it may be asked, have particular ones been chosen and not others? Should collegiality have been included? The reason it was not selected is that, as a virtue this disposition is, perhaps, more important in certain bioscience disciplines, where there is greater emphasis on teamwork than in others such as history or philosophy where the lone researcher may still prosper. Despite the dominance of principalism, many of the virtues identified in this chapter do actually appear in the text of research codes. The appearance of these virtues, however, needs to be searched for. They are often buried away and they are not treated with the headline prominence given to principles derived from the Georgetown mantra.

The importance of researchers demonstrating trust, truthfulness, or honesty may be found in most research codes. Mention of virtuous qualities appears, for example, in the UK Medical Research Council position statement on research regulation and ethics (2006). They may also be found in the research ethics statements of professional or discipline-based societies such as the American Anthropological Association (1998) or the American Psychological Association (2002). Accuracy, another component of the virtue of sincerity (see chapter 7), is a quality incorporated by the UK Economic and Social Research Council (ESRC) in its research ethics framework (2006). The ESRC framework also notes the importance of researchers exercising openness. Even allusions to reflexive awareness are occasionally made, such as in a Europe-wide code of practice for socio-economic research (Respect, 2006). Support for the incorporation of some consideration of virtue ethics has been growing. This has been reflected in the way that Beauchamp and Childress have gradually expanded consideration of the role of the virtues in later editions of their book about bio-medical ethics.

It is notable that some degree of consensus surrounds the importance of dispositions such as truthfulness, impartiality, and openness. But while such virtuous dispositions are mentioned in codes of research ethics they are rarely noted more than in passing. Hence, virtues often appear in codes of research ethics but this is rarely, if ever, accompanied by any serious attempt to explain what they are intended to mean in practice.

The word "integrity" is perhaps the excellence of character which appears most often in codes of practice and admonitions to behave "well." However, while it is frequently asserted it is rarely, if ever, explained. But what, exactly, does integrity mean? There are many different meanings attached to this word (Fjellstrom, 2005). The root of integrity derives from the Latin words "*integer*" and "*integritas*" meaning whole or entire. This suggests that integrity is about integrating different parts of one's own true self, physically, mentally, and perhaps socially. It is about developing an integrated identity as a person or possibly as a professional person fulfilling such functions. From a legal standpoint, Fjellstrom (2005) suggests that integrity may be further interpreted as meaning the possession of certain rights, such as those associated with being a citizen or owning property. One should not violate the "integrity" of a person's privacy or private property, for example. Beauchamp and Childress (1989, 35) refer to the "integrity of rules," for instance. Finally, integrity can be understood as respecting the intrinsic worth of each individual and their human dignity. This is an interpretation that may be found in declarations pertaining to human rights agreed by multinational bodies such as the European

Union (Fjellstrom, 2005). This defines integrity in terms of respect for the individual and all other life forms.

Seeking to explain and explore what integrity means for the contemporary researcher is, in essence, the task of this book. In doing this I am principally adopting the idea of integrity as the integration of a person's true self and linking their values and identity as a person with their practice as a researcher. I believe that this constitutes a "gap" in our understanding about research ethics which I am seeking to fill through identifying virtues that particularly relate to the research process.

CONCLUSION

The virtues and vices presented for the first time in this chapter will form the focus of the second section of the book. Each subsequent chapter will explore one of these virtues and its attendant vice in detail, sometimes drawing on short narratives of ethical issues provided by researchers in a range of disciplines. The choice of virtues associated with different stages of the research process is intended to be illustrative rather than prescriptive. There is no suggestion that other virtues may not also be pertinent to the research process, but those chosen provide a framework for discussing a virtue-based approach to research ethics. It also does not imply that virtues such as respectfulness or sincerity do not operate across many if not all phases of research to some extent. But identifying moral virtues that have particular resonance for each stage of research is a way of shining a light on the link between our practice and our moral character. The implications of living these virtues out in practice will be the focus of the second section of this book.

PART TWO

LIVING THE VIRTUES

The second section of the book will focus on developing an understanding of the moral virtues (and vices) outlined toward the end of the last chapter. To be meaningful, these virtues need to be explored in more detail and "lived out" in practice. This is a very personal challenge rather than one that can be monitored by a code of practice or a committee. If a virtue cannot be understood in this way, it will become little more than a meaningless mantra or "hurrah" word.

This section will also draw on a number of short narratives provided by academic researchers from a range of disciplines such as accountancy, archaeology, chemistry, economics, education, environmental science, history, law, management, mathematics, and social work. These are candid accounts of ethical issues that worry real-life researchers. The contributors reflect on making good and bad choices and how their personality and beliefs impact on the way they conduct their research. The narratives illustrate the uncertainties that many, even quite experienced, researchers have about issues they face "in the field." Some are written by quite senior professors; others have been contributed by more inexperienced researchers just beginning their academic careers. They provide a candid insight into the doubts that confront researchers in their everyday work. These narratives are central to the purpose of the book in seeking to demonstrate that, unless the discussion of virtue is embedded in the real experience of the researcher, this approach may quickly slide into an agreeable but essentially empty set of smug-sounding adjectives.

4

COURAGE

Courageous research is the only kind of research that matters.
(Walkerdine, 2003, 129)

INTRODUCTION

As we saw in the last chapter, the research process is often described as a
"journey." Starting out on any journey can be exciting. There is the
thrill of anticipation, looking forward to new experiences that bring
the promise of fresh insights about the world. For some of us, we may
be planning to go to destinations we have long dreamed of or admired,
to understand more about somewhere or something. We may feel pas-
sionately interested in our intended destination or simply have an idle
curiosity. The rest of us may be making a return to a favorite destination but still in the hope of learning more about it. This sense of
anticipation and excitement though is often tempered by a different,
less positive emotion: one of fear of the unknown. Researchers starting
out on a new investigation or major project can share a similar set of
mixed emotions. Like the intrepid traveller they are going on an
exploration into the unknown. The destination holds out the promise
of intellectual riches but also demands the moral virtue of *courage* to
take on a significant research challenge.

THE OPEN ROAD

The fear of failure is with us in life and never more so than when
undertaking a piece of academic research. It takes courage to tackle new
challenges or problems, or to frame fresh questions or hypotheses.

While researchers seek to set parameters on what they are trying to find out this is still no guarantee of ultimate success. In designing investigations researchers face early choices that demand courage. How challenging should the research question or problem be? Will it be rooted in one discipline or traverse several cognate fields? To what extent will it rely on established theoretical or methodological perspectives? Is this going to be a short-term piece of work or a longitudinal study possibly taking many years of hard work to complete? But perhaps most challenging of all is the question as to whether, as a researcher, one feels capable of succeeding. Do we, in other words, feel that we possess the intellectual and physical resources to accomplish our objective? Ultimately, doing research means putting yourself "on the line." It is about risking failure.

Another issue is that a particular line of enquiry or topic might be out of fashion or simply be positively discouraged. It might be considered not just unfashionable but politically or socially controversial. There are societal problems which are also "taboo" subjects: child abuse, gene therapy, or exploring the cognitive differences between men and women serve as obvious examples. Here, it takes courage to undertake investigations into unpopular or controversial topics. In such circumstances, suspicions may attach to the motivation of the researcher. At the extreme, those undertaking research into such social issues may be accused of voyeurism or acting irresponsibly in applying a rational, scientific perspective in an attempt to understand or explain behavior labelled by society as beyond the bounds of decency. However, what is considered taboo can vary across cultures and also change rapidly within cultures. Charles Darwin's work on natural selection is a good example of research which was taboo in its time, since it appeared to challenge fundamental Christian beliefs about the way the world was created (see later in this chapter).

While some research topics may be taboo, certain forms of research may be considered of less value or lower in status within the academic community. "Pedagogic research," where academics and other teachers systematically investigate and reflect on aspects of teaching theory and practice, is said to be an example of this phenomenon. Some of this work does result in well-respected peer-reviewed publications, while it can also include "nothing more than new insights informing an individual's practice" (Stierer, 2007, 1). Moreover, pedagogic research has tended to be marginalized and treated as of less importance than research into the disciplines. This has been reinforced by audit exercises designed to judge the quality of academic research output in a UK context. This means that dedicating one's effort to the pursuit of pedagogic research has been characterized as "a form of career suicide" or a "booby prize" only undertaken by those who are perceived as incapable of undertaking disciplinary research (Stierer, 2007, 2). Hence, research involves a personal investment of not just time but an emotional commitment to a form of investigation that may not necessarily be of benefit to one's academic career. Making a decision to pursue such a line of enquiry takes courage.

While courage is required at many stages of the research process, such as in overcoming obstacles whilst gathering data or ideas (see chapter 6), it is particularly pertinent at the earliest phase involving the framing of the research. This involves determining the scope of the research and making choices about how demanding (or ambitious) the project will be. A doctoral student may spend anything up to a year framing and reframing research questions or problems. Here, the researcher needs to decide through which one of Flecker's "Gates of Damascus" he or she will travel. To return to the metaphor, described by Delamont (see chapter 3), some of these gates represent more risk to the researcher than others. The Aleppo Gate is for trade and commerce and may represent a funded or contract research project. Here, a funding body or agency will normally be seeking clear answers to research questions which relate to agendas primarily motivated by profit. Hence, the researcher will need to satisfy more than his or her own intellectual curiosity. The results will be scrutinized for the extent to which they represent good value and their fitness for the purpose for which the work was sponsored. Another of Flecker's "safer" exits is the Mecca Gate. This is for devotees of a particular methodological or ideological faith. Here, the researcher has the security of pursuing a familiar methodological or ideological perspective. This may be through adhering to a methodology which represents an established way of undertaking a research investigation in the discipline rather than adopting one that breaks with or challenges received wisdom.

There are other gates that represent more bold or courageous routes into the unknown. These are the Baghdad and the Lebanon Gates. They are more challenging and dangerous exits. The Baghdad Gate is for the truly daring who are prepared to take on projects which can be difficult, lonely, and dangerous. It is for those prepared to take greater intellectual risks where the odds of success may be stacked against them but the possibility of glory is too tempting to resist. Some research can be not only intellectually "risky" but physically dangerous. Anthropologists can face particular risks to their physical safety and well-being as part of the research process, especially when researching crime, working in war zones, or in other politically unstable or violent environments (Lee-Treweek & Linkogle, 2000). The environment may also carry medical risks to the researcher. Adriana Petryna, a medical anthropologist, spent 18 months conducting research in the Ukraine on the effects of the 1986 Chernobyl nuclear explosion which is estimated to have led to well over half a million people being exposed to radiation. This work carried the personal risk of exposure to cancer-causing radiation for the researcher (Petryna, 2002).

However, the Lebanon Gate is the riskiest one of all for the researcher. Delamont (2005, 89) explains the attraction and the dangers of the Lebanon Gate for researchers in the education field in the following terms:

> The Lebanon Gate is the high risk and high reward alternative. Many educational researchers never choose the Lebanon Gate because it exposes us to risk. We could lose our epistemological certainties, our standpoints, our methodological foundations, and we could be forced to find new literatures, new theories, new perspectives on education itself.

While Delamont uses Flecker's poem as an extended metaphor for research into education it is really applicable to researchers in any field. Becoming a researcher is about opening oneself up to new knowledge and new possibilities. Some directions of travel can entail challenging conventional boundaries and reshaping one's own identity in the process.

CHALLENGING BOUNDARIES

In *Courageous Research* (Martin & Booth, 2003), Elaine Martin argues that research may be regarded as "courageous" for one of three reasons. Firstly, it may deploy research methods which are not widely understood or accepted within the context of a discipline; secondly, the research may be considered "audacious" possibly in challenging orthodox or established perspectives; and, thirdly, where the commitment of research students to a particular study comes "of the heart." Being courageous takes considerable emotional energy. The Latin root of courage, *cor*, meaning heart, is echoed in our phrase "take heart."

The advance of scientific understanding about the world has depended on individuals prepared to endure criticism and sometimes personal danger to contradict orthodoxies of their time. Galileo's astronomical observations challenged the prevailing idea of his time that the sun, and other planets, revolved around the earth and that the earth was the center of the universe. The English physician William

Harvey faced considerable opposition to his claims about the circulation of the blood around the body during the early seventeenth century largely because he contradicted the widely established ideas of Galen. As a result of Harvey's claims his own medical practice suffered and it took many years for his research to become accepted (Smiles, 1910). Similarly, the research of Charles Darwin on the origin of species was considered highly controversial for establishing the scientific theory of evolution based on a process of natural selection. This appeared to contradict conventional Biblical faith, based on the first chapter of Genesis, that God created every living creature. The conclusions reached by Darwin and subsequent evolutionary biologists remain the subject of opposition from Creationists to this day.

Occasionally, a researcher, such as Darwin, will bring about a fundamental change in the way that people understand and interpret the world. This is what is commonly referred to as a "paradigm shift," a phrase coined by Thomas Kuhn (1962) who argued that over time a change takes place in the way "one conceptual world view is replaced by another" as a result of a "series of peaceful interludes punctuated by intellectually violent revolutions" (1962, 10). A paradigm can be understood by reference to what is thought worth observing or scrutinizing, the type of questions pursued, and the interpretation of results from subsequent investigations. Some researchers work within conventional paradigms or dominant understandings about the world while others set out to challenge received wisdom. The influence of the scientific method is such that many contemporary researchers see the adoption of alternative methodologies as essential to advancing their field of enquiry.

Dominant understandings about the world are also shaped by the boundaries of academic disciplines. It takes courage to decide to conduct a research project that cuts across established disciplinary boundaries. Some research topics traverse disciplines more than others. A good example is suicidology, which is concerned with understanding the nature, causes, and prevention of suicide deploying the behavioral sciences. Researching suicide brings together a range of disciplines cutting across the natural, social, and applied sciences including biology, sociology, psychiatry, psychology, economics, and neurochemistry (Webb, 2003). For any researcher, this is a demanding and complex set of disciplines to bring to bear on a subject that is also taboo or unfashionable. There are many other research topics which are vital in understanding the modern world but which cannot be neatly ascribed to just one discipline. Examples include globalization, both as a phenomenon and in its social and economic effects, or the causes and possible resolution of world poverty. In seeking to understand poverty a wide variety of disciplinary perspectives are critical including agriculture, politics, sociology, economics, and environmental science among many others.

THE "COST" OF RESEARCH

We often think of learning, whether through being taught or via independent enquiry, as referring to the process of adding to our existing stock of knowledge, skills, or attitudes. However, learning is not always about trying to "know more" based on our existing knowledge and beliefs. Learning can be "supplantive" as well as "additive" (Atherton, 2003). This means, whether we realize it or not, replacing our existing stock of knowledge and beliefs with new ones. This can prove a personally painful process as we may be reluctant to abandon our old beliefs about the world with a fresh set of ideas. Learning, in other words, can have a "cost" (Atherton, 2003). This is about challenging our own sense of identity of who we are (or ontology) as much as what we "know" (or epistemology). In a similar vein, other writers have identified that some knowledge can prove "troublesome" or challenging to understand conceptually or emotionally (Meyer & Land, 2006). This can mean that learners are caught in a state of "liminality" between existing knowledge and values and a new set of concepts or belief system. This is about more than a simple, quantitative cognitive shift. It can involve a repositioning of self. In other words, developing as a learner is about knowing who you are as much as producing new knowledge (Barnett, 2007).

In the narrative entitled "crossing the boundary" (see narrative 4.1), an experienced academic decided to change direction in late career to undertake research in history. The narrative expresses the various hurdles this researcher has faced in undertaking a research degree and the "fear of failure" about starting academic work in a new field. In many respects, part of this person's discomfort is about being in a state of liminality, caught between a previous identity in business and management studies and their new, emerging identity as a historian.

Narrative 4.1

Crossing the Boundary

At a very late stage in my academic career, I decided to make a fresh start in a new academic discipline—history. This was primarily motivated by personal interest coupled with a desire to research and publish in the field. On reflection, there was an element of rashness and possibly conceit in my decision since I seriously underestimated the challenges involved in adjusting to the intellectual and methodological demands of a discipline that was significantly different from the one in which I had spent much of my previous career in academia—business and management. Put another way, I did not fully appreciate what was involved in crossing the boundary from one academic discipline to another. Thus, I struggled to find the "right voice" with which to communicate my ideas and to engage with confidence in the discourse of history. As a result, I modified my original intention of registering for a doctorate and opted for a master's in research instead. Once I had completed my master's degree, however, I turned my attention to preparing a research proposal for a doctorate. Notwithstanding my eventual success at master's level, I was still extremely diffident about this, a concern which was well founded since my initial attempt was severely criticized for being too vague and lacking in historiographical rigor. At this point, I nearly threw in the towel. However, I swallowed my pride and produced a revised version of my proposal which was far more favorably received. I then encountered a further hurdle, namely that my intended supervisor did not feel he had the appropriate expertise in my chosen field of research and he suggested that I look elsewhere. This was totally unexpected and I was somewhat daunted by the prospect of having to approach other academics to supervise my research. At the time of writing, the challenge of finding someone suitable has not been fully met. Throughout this experience, there has always been, at the back of my mind, the fear of failure and of not being fully accepted by members of the academic community that I have been seeking to join. It is proving to be a long haul and as yet there is no guarantee of ultimate success.

Writers such as Meyer, Land and Atherton have focused their attention on understanding learning mainly from a teaching rather than a research perspective. However, the notion of the "cost" of learning and the state of liminality between prior and emerging understanding is just as relevant to the research process. Courage in research may also be thought of as facing personal fears and overcoming these as part of the internal life of the mind, as illustrated in the narrative. While the analogy of research as a journey of transformation is often made there may be elements to this journey which raise fears of loss as well as gain. This can involve a changing sense of identity (Green, 2005). A good example is provided by a group of research students undertaking doctoral degrees in art and design which formed the particular focus of a study by Jacquelyn Collinson (2005). She identified that novice researchers in art and design were fearful of laying bare their "routines of creativity" (p720). At worst, researchers feared that exposing their creative processes to scrutiny, rather than just their products, might damage their future capacity to be creative or innovative. This resulted from a perception that creativity is a fragile and essentially private process that might be lost if opened up to explicit scrutiny. Possessing doubts about the impact of the research process on one's own creative or intellectual identity demands a leap of faith. It also means letting go of previous, perhaps strongly held conceptions of personal and professional identity in the process.

Another example of courage in abandoning a strongly held belief which formed part of the researcher's identity is provided by the case of John Colquhoun, a dental practitioner and researcher who later became the Principal Dental Officer in Auckland, the largest city in New Zealand. Through his dental education and training, Colquhoun developed a strong belief in the efficacy of adding fluoride to the water supply. In his own words, he was an "ardent supporter" (Colquhoun, 1997, 29) of fluoridation both through his research and, later, as an influential public spokesperson for his profession. He published a research paper in the *New Zealand Dental Journal* which argued that fluoridation had helped to stem tooth decay in children, especially those from low income families (Colquhoun, 1977). However, in his role as Principal Dental Officer he came to have growing doubts about the wisdom of fluoridation. He came across a study that indicated that child dental health was actually better in non-fluoridated areas in New Zealand. Other international studies started to indicate that there was virtually no significant statistical relationship between tooth decay and water fluoride. At the same time, he started to question the results of other researchers who were convinced of the benefits of fluoridation, particularly in respect to the way population samples were selected. Additionally, other studies indicated that fluoride could cause degenerative damage to teeth as well as the bones of elderly people. He then published his own study that reported that 25% of children in the city of Auckland had dental fluorosis, a condition that refers to damage and discoloration to teeth (Colquhoun, 1984).

Colquhoun saw his fundamental beliefs challenged by new research and experienced regret that he had been scornful of those who had first opposed fluoridation. He had had to "unlearn" his established beliefs about the relationship between fluoride and dental health. In an article explaining why he changed his mind about water fluoridation he refers to the way that he resisted abandoning his old beliefs.

I now realize that what my colleagues and I were doing was what the history of science shows all professionals do when their pet theory is confronted by disconcerting new evidence: they bend over backwards to explain away the new evidence. They try very hard to keep their theory intact—especially so if their own professional reputations depend on maintaining that theory. (Colquhoun, 1997, 30)

As Colquhoun makes clear, the difficulty in accepting this new research was that it challenged him on both an ontological as well as an epistemological level. It was a brave step for anyone to break from the weight of accepted opinion—that fluoride was positively linked to dental health. In doing so, he had to risk his established reputation which was based on the promotion of fluoridation.

I now realize that I had learned, in my training in dentistry, only one side of the scientific controversy over fluoridation. I had been taught, and believed, that there was really no scientific case against fluoridation, and that only misinformed lay people and a few crackpot professionals were foolish enough to oppose it . . . I do not believe that the selection and bias that apparently occurred was necessarily deliberate. Enthusiasts for a theory can fool themselves very often, and persuade themselves and others that their activities are genuinely scientific. I am also aware that, after 50 years of widespread acceptance and endorsement of fluoridation, many scholars (including the reviewers of this essay) may find it difficult to accept the claim that the original fluoridation studies were invalid. (Colquhoun, 1997, 31)

As the example of fluoridation illustrates, research is a continuous process and projects, whether undertaken as individuals or in teams, rarely produce all the answers. This means that the researcher must have the courage to live with doubt and uncertainty. They may be able to provide some of the possible answers but rarely all of them with any conviction. Courageous researchers need a quality that the poet John Keats called negative capability. This means that rational answers to questions and problems are not always available and that this means we must live with being in a state of uncertainty. While researchers may strive to get answers to their questions, they must also accept that they may not be able to generate complete understanding and cope with continuing doubt.

Part of the uncertainty of research is how one's own work will be understood, interpreted, and applied. This can be beneficial to mankind or may have consequences which are entirely unanticipated. Research may have unintended consequences, both good and bad. Albert Einstein's theory of relativity, for example, helped lay the scientific foundations for the creation of the atomic bomb even though he was personally committed to peace and disarmament and uninvolved in the subsequent application of his work for destructive purposes.

WHEN COURAGE FAILS

Like all virtues, courage is a mean between extremes. A lack of courage is normally represented by the vice of *cowardice*. In research terms, cowardice may be interpreted as being unwilling to tackle big or important questions, as shying away from difficult or unknown intellectual terrain for fear of failure or being too easily contented with the answers one is receiving in response to a research question. Some types of research may demand more courage than others. In seeking out answers to theoretical or "why" questions, researchers may rub up against conventional responses or theories that currently purport to explain a phenomenon. Asking "why?" frequently entails questioning the taken-for-granted. On the other hand, other research projects may have more limited intellectual ambitions. Rather than questioning received wisdom they may seek to be more practical in orientation, considering "how to" implement a system, process, or procedure. This does not necessarily mean that someone possesses insufficient courage but that the nature of the research project is more limited and therefore requires them to exercise less courage, Furthermore, if the findings challenge conventional wisdom it may still require courage to champion them.

We need to be courageous in facing up critically to the task of trying to understand our own taken-for-granted assumptions. Failure to do so can lead to research which, advertently or inadvertently, becomes a self-fulfilling prophecy (Merton, 1948). This phrase means that when a situation is falsely defined it can lead to behavior that ultimately makes the false definition come true. Merton gave a number of examples of the self-fulfilling prophecy. One of these concerns the collapse of a bank in the 1930s. While the bank was perfectly solvent at the start of the day an unfounded rumor circulated that it was on the verge of bankruptcy. This led to investors panicking and withdrawing their savings, resulting in the collapse of the bank by the end of the day since it did not have sufficient liquid assets to pay its customers. What had been a false rumor at the beginning of the day had become true because people believed it to be the case. Merton also gave the example of a teacher who is told that his new pupils are highly intelligent. As a result of such information, which may or may not be true, the teacher's expectations about their students will be raised, resulting in the award of higher grades. Similarly, the reverse will occur if the teacher is told that their new pupils have low intelligence. Their expectations of low achievement will become a self-fulfilling prophecy. This phenomenon was the subject of a book by Rosenthal and Jacobson called *Pygmalion in the Classroom* (1968). In their book Rosenthal and Jacobson argued that the "labelling" of school students as having social or intellectual disadvantages has an (adverse) impact on the expectations of teachers.

In practical terms, hypotheses can become self-fulfilling. This means we need to try our best to put aside our "hunches," otherwise we risk simply confirming our existing frameworks or prejudices. This is more easily said than done though and takes both courage and reflexivity about oneself (see chapter 9). In some science disciplines methodological convention is partly designed to guard against the possibility of designing a self-fulfilling hypothesis. The development of "blind" and "double blind" experiments are intended to cut out the bias of the researcher through ensuring that the research subject, and sometimes both the subject and the researcher, are unaware that they are part of an experimental group receiving a new drug or treatment or part of a control group receiving a placebo. The difficulty for the social researcher is that they may often have a personal "investment" in the research that makes it hard for them to put aside their assumptions and prejudices. We can have dispositions and find ourselves in particular situations that make it difficult not to fall into the trap of the self-fulfilling prophecy. A researcher with strong religious convictions might be considered to have a disposition or bias if he or she decided to undertake research into the importance of religion in modern secular society. Similarly, a researcher who is part of the phenomenon they are studying may fall foul of situation bias, such as an educational researcher who is also working as a school teacher or university lecturer. Their social location makes the possibility of such bias a clear risk. This is a major criticism of so-called "action research" where the researcher is also part of the phenomenon and able to shape the change process within the organization in which they are working.

THE RECKLESS RESEARCHER

Cowardice to take on a challenging research question or task is at one end of the spectrum. At the other end is recklessness in taking on a project which is beyond one's own intellectual or practical capabilities. Narrative 4.1 reflects a researcher's anxiety that he might not be capable of achieving the task he had set for himself. This is an understandable fear for anyone beginning a new research project, especially one in an intellectual area where the researcher is a comparative novice. At a practical level, a research project needs to be "do-able" in the time-frame you have available. In this sense, all research involves a degree of compromise. While this is not necessarily intellectual in nature there are practical considerations connected with time, money, and resources. Some projects can be too large or ambitious in scope for one researcher to cope with alone. Teamwork is common in the sciences where large data sets, expensive equipment, time-consuming laboratory tests, and the demands of double blind clinical trials necessitate collaboration.

Recklessness might manifest itself in other ways through a lack of intellectual groundwork. Some researchers simply start a project insufficiently prepared in terms of the extent to which they have read and understood the literature in their field. Here, the most obvious danger is that the same, or a relevantly similar piece of research, may have already been completed. This can result in a researcher being unaware that they are repeating a previous investigation. The importance of ensuring that one is well grounded in the literature is demonstrated in all scholarly work through a literature review. It is customary for a literature review of some description to precede the development of the investigatory phase of any research. The format of most research articles and theses will also contain such a section or chapter. This enables the researcher to demonstrate that their investigation is well founded on an understanding and analysis of previous scholarly work.

A reckless approach can have adverse implications for human research subjects, such as designing a set of research questions which may be unnecessarily intrusive or even offensive. This type of problem can occur when insufficient thought is given to research design issues or there has not been a "pilot" phase, the intention of which is to refine questions, problems, or hypotheses before serious data collection begins. This links closely with respectfulness in the treatment of human subjects which will be the focus of the next chapter.

CONCLUSION

Doing research is both an intellectual and an emotional challenge. While the importance of taking intellectual risks in asking difficult questions and testing out received wisdom is widely acknowledged, it is less often understood as an emotionally demanding process of "letting go" of our own assumptions about the world. Researchers need the ability to deal with their own emotions if they are to have the courage needed to pursue a demanding and ultimately worthwhile project. Courage is also needed to cope with the road ahead and the disappointments and frustrations that can occur along the way.

5

RESPECTFULNESS

A virtuous act is one in which the ends of self and of the other are respected and promoted jointly. (Adler, 1918, 214)

INTRODUCTION

Respectfulness is a virtue which is equally applicable in both qualitative and quantitative research (Willig, 2001). It demands treating research subjects "with respect." This often results in a set of negative injunctions. Researchers are told they must *not* deceive their human subjects as to the purpose of their project. Another routine expectation is *not* to reveal the identity of research subjects in subsequent reporting or to use material collected for reasons other than originally intended. However, respectfulness also implies positive actions such as informing research subjects of their right to withdraw permission to use data about them at any stage. Other positive actions might include giving research subjects some follow-up information about what the study has found out, and actively maintaining confidentiality with regard to their involvement and information stored about them. Respectfulness means treating a research subject as a person rather than simply as a resource to be exploited.

MORE THAN A MANTRA

As we have seen, most, if not all, codes of research conduct are strongly focused on the importance of respect as a *principle* rather than respectfulness as a moral *virtue*. In this regard, they follow Kant's categorical imperative as a rational principle. The logic of reversibility involves considering whether one would be prepared to have one's own actions brought to bear on oneself. In practice, though, this proposition might justify mistreatment of a research subject if a researcher attached limited importance to their own treatment under similar circumstances. At the extreme, for example, a racist might support the idea that black or Jewish people can be mistreated even if they were a member of such a race themselves. However, demonstrating this disposition as a *virtue* requires the exercise of sensitivity toward all those affected by the research process, notably human subjects as well as animals, rather than a theoretical declaration that one will follow this principle. It is about respecting the right to life, to informed consent and to privacy, and *living out* this virtue in practice.

Living out the virtue of respectfulness is not as easy as it might sound. Here, confidentiality and anonymity need to be more than mantras contained in research proposals or communications with research subjects. It is routine to promise to keep everything a research subject might say confidential and ensure their identity remains a secret. Keeping this promise can be a lot harder, especially where a study is drawing on a small community of individuals many of whom may know each other. A good example of how difficult it is to live out the virtue of respectfulness is provided in a narrative contributed by an educational researcher (see narrative 5.1).

Narrative 5.1

The Complexities of "Confidentiality"

I find that most of the dilemmas that exercise me are ones that receive scant attention in the methodological literature or in "how to do research" books. If they are addressed, they are presented as relatively unproblematic issues that can be resolved by following "ethical guidelines" that protect both our sources and our integrity. This proves a far more challenging balancing act in practice.

One unwarranted assurance that comes to mind is that of "confidentiality." It is on rare occasions that, as researchers, we really offer anybody confidentiality in the commonly understood sense of the term—other than with explicitly "off the record" contributions. We intend to disclose (by paraphrasing, citing, or quoting) what we have been told, once data is verified and permission given. I've had to clarify that distinction to one of my potential respondents who queried the terms of the guarantees in my lengthy letter negotiating access. I've had cause to reword my letters to avoid the suggestion of unwarranted guarantees. It has caused to me to think more deeply about the nature of confidentiality, anonymity, and respect for sources—some of whom are powerful and in need of little protection but others are in far more vulnerable positions.

One particular dilemma exercises me at the moment in my own research, namely dealing with the risk, or rather the inevitability, of deductive disclosure. I'm doing multi-site case study research, in a small number of institutions in a small country where the number of such institutions is relatively small. In spite of my best efforts to anonymize my sites, projects, and respondents (using aliases, codes, and general role descriptors) any informed reader would have little difficulty identifying the sites, even the individual respondents. Deductive disclosure is a real concern. I'm assured by others (such as my supervisor) that these people, given their professional roles, are not naïve and have verified their transcripts in full knowledge of my intention to cite/or quote them. I'm not so sure, however, if they fully comprehend the potential consequences, especially as multiple (and often conflicting) perspectives are offered by different respondents—for example at different levels of seniority within one site. Maybe I'm being over-sensitive.

As a consequence, I have decided that each individual respondent will verify (and amend if necessary) their *own* transcript. It seems neither feasible nor desirable to give them, collectively, the opportunity to review (or verify or otherwise) the case study report. In an ideal world, I might have considered getting all of them around the table to hear their response to my report—my interpretation of "what is going on here." But I believe that some respondents have offered certain insights on the (tacit) understanding that they would be "kind of confidential." I believe that while they expect to be cited/quoted anonymously they do not expect to have their contribution shared with others, as would be the case when contributors read a single case study report.

So I'm trying to devise a strategy of writing minimalist case study vignettes (for the body of the thesis) and presenting confidential extended case study appendices for the examiners, with the more readily identifiable details. It's certainly not ideal. I have merely deferred, however, dealing with the more fundamental issue at stake. How to report case study research (which draws on multiple perspectives) without betraying the implicit expectation of "confidentiality"? I'm reluctant to rock the boat by exploring in too much detail, unless asked, what they actually understand by "anonymity." I've spelt it out in writing, and they *seem* to realize what they are signing up to. Still keeps me awake at night though! The problem is compounded by the fact that I know many of my participants, professionally and in some cases even personally. I console myself that once it's bound in covers and on the shelf of a university in a distant land, that no one (including my respondents) will bother to read it. But then there's another part of me that wants it to make a bit of

> a difference. And already some have asked for a copy when it's done! As
> if life wasn't complicated enough . . .

The narrative illustrates how difficult it can be in practice to protect the identity of research subjects. The concern of the researcher is that "deductive disclosure" might occur where it would be easy for someone to guess the identity of a research subject. However, the researcher is also conscious of the fact that the research subjects are her professional peers. This means, among other things, that they are likely to be more informed about the research process itself and understand the consequences of participation. In short, their education and position as peers means that their consent is probably quite "informed," or, in other words, based on a fuller understanding of the implications of participating in the study. However, despite the status of her subjects, and the reassurances of her supervisor, the researcher is still anxious that identities may be deduced or guessed, resulting in unintended consequences. Transforming colleagues into research subjects is quite common among professionals pursuing research degrees, such as teachers or social workers, and demands more attention than it has erstwhile been given. Here, there are calls for an ethic of "care" in order to safeguard moral and personal relations (Costley & Gibbs, 2006).

Being able to persuade research subjects (or "participants") to disclose information about themselves and others involves skill and patience. Here, women are sometimes thought to be better able to persuade research subjects to be candid and also to develop greater "rapport" with participants from both sexes in the process (Warren, 1988). Achieving disclosure demands good communication skills and what is sometimes described as an "unthreatening" demeanor. Being a successful researcher also brings with it a particular responsibility not to breach the trust upon which the relationship with the research subject is based. "Sensitive" research topics such as HIV/AIDS, suicide, or bereavement are among the most important (Lee, 1993). They also require particular care in developing relationships with research subjects. Writing from a feminist perspective, Lather (1986) identifies "rape research" as investigatory practices that alienate or exploit research subjects. In this context, "rape research" does not refer to the investigation of sexual crimes normally committed against women. Rather, it refers to the temptation to use research subjects in an exploitative way without any consideration as to the consequences for those who have contributed to data or information-gathering.

Interpreted in a broader context, "rape research" may also refer to the exploitation of the knowledge base of indigenous peoples or the physical environment for both economic gain and personal glorification (see narrative 5.2). In some national settings protection of indigenous peoples is built into the framework of research governance. In New Zealand, for example, the active protection of the rights and lands of the Maori people is enshrined in the Treaty of Waitangi dating back to the nineteenth century. In a contemporary context this means that research codes of New Zealand higher education institutions, such as Massey University, include a requirement for research to be carried out in a socially and culturally sensitive manner with due regard for the Maori people.

Respectfulness as a virtue is closely linked with an awareness on the part of the researcher of potential and real inequalities in power relationships. The existence of unequal power relations makes the possibility of an abuse of informed consent more real. Researchers need to take particular care in developing country contexts where research subjects may suffer from poverty and a lack of literacy that can affect communication and, hence, full informed consent. This consideration can extend to contexts where there are vast disparities of wealth, such as South Africa. Here, linguistic and cultural diversity makes it ethically challenging to obtain genuine informed consent (Louw & Delport, 2006). The legacy of apartheid also means that researchers tend to be disproportionately white, and drawn from socially and educationally privileged backgrounds (Louw & Delport, 2006). Equality issues concern particular disciplinary specialists. Ethnobotanists, for example, who study relationships between plants and peoples, need to be sensitive to the extent to which their work might take advantage of the intellectual property of aboriginal peoples with respect to herbal medicines. Knowledge of such treatments has great commercial potential for drug companies but can lead to accusations of "biopiracy" (Gutterman, 2006).

The work of researchers in some disciplines, such as anthropology, environmental science, and archaeology, necessitates a particular sensitivity toward and respect for cultures and fragile environments. Moreover, while respectfulness is normally interpreted as demonstrating consideration and due regard for people living in the present it is also connected with the impact of our research work on future generations. For example, scientists whose work has an impact on the physical environment may feel the need to consider whether their efforts to understand the nature of our natural surroundings could, inadvertently, contribute to the degradation of the place they are researching (see narrative 5.2).

Narrative 5.2

Experimenting with the Environment

I undertook my PhD research in one of the last few pristine, uninhabitable areas on earth: the High Arctic. My studies were to investigate the plant communities that grew there and to explore the potential impacts of predicted climate change scenarios, such as warmer temperatures, more rainfall, and increased nutrient levels.

My research was part of a larger national project, working and collecting samples within a protected reserve where we had permission to do this from the relevant authorities of the nation state. It wasn't until the second or third year of fieldwork that the impact of the research I was doing on the natural environment began to sit uneasily with me. It struck me that in order to provide evidence on the fragility of the communities I was studying, I was actively damaging them. As my reading and knowledge of other researchers' work broadened and deepened, I began to feel uneasy about repeating experimental work that clearly had a locally destructive and long-lasting effect. By the end of my research, I was modifying the approaches as far as possible to have the least impact on the environment while still being able to answer the questions I had posed. While I continued to believe in the need for research and evidence to protect the environment, I couldn't reconcile my own and others research approaches with this: it simply felt hypocritical.

I undertook my PhD work (it shocks me to think!) 12 years ago. Last year, after three years of applying for funding, I received a university-funded scholarship for a studentship to use mathematical modelling approaches with existing data sets from destructive sampling experiments in the Arctic work. The student is now looking at models that best fit the data and forecast the likely impacts on these fragile communities of climate change predictions. This project is dear to my heart as 12 years after my work, the same approaches and measurements are taking place: in the same reserve where I worked and in many others. How much more of this data is needed to demonstrate that these communities are easily damaged? Hopefully my student's work will add a new perspective on the value of these data.

Understanding the dimensions of respectfulness as a virtue are complex and demand awareness and sensitivity to local cultural contexts. Much has been written about the difference between Eastern and Western culture and this literature often emphasizes the collectivist nature of Eastern societies such as Japan where, in contrast with Western cultural norms, the needs of the group are often elevated above those of the individual. "Respectfulness" means a lot more than respecting the needs and interests of the individual but extends to the community, group, or family to which the person belongs. In practical terms this may mean that the researcher needs to consult with the community to gain their consent rather than simply approaching an individual and seeking their "consent" (Benatar, 2002). The difference between Western and Eastern attitudes to respectfulness may be illustrated by practices surrounding organ donation in Japan (Akabayashi & Slingsby, 2003). In the West, donor cards provide evidence of an individual's consent to donate their organs for human transplantation on their death. However, the importance of the family in Japanese society led to the creation of donor cards that allow the donor's family to withdraw permission. The importance of the family in Japanese society also affects the disclosure practices of doctors when treating patients with serious illnesses. The withholding of information from individuals about their medical condition is a well-established practice among Japanese doctors especially when patients have a poor prognosis or have a psychiatric illness (Powell, 2006). The motivation behind non-disclosure again lies in what Fetters (1998) terms "family autonomy." Here, a patient's family may be informed of their condition rather than the individual. This is intended to show respect for the role of the family in shielding a loved one from hurtful information. Clearly, Japanese norms give a higher standing to the concerns of the family contrasting with Western attitudes which stress the primacy of individual autonomy. The researcher needs to be cognizant of such cultural considerations in interpreting and adequately contextualizing the meaning of respectfulness.

MANIPULATIVENESS

Gaining access to and information from research subjects is essential to many forms of research. Without data from research subjects research projects will often fail. This fact can tempt the researcher to cut corners in dealing with research subjects and, in extreme cases, result in the vice of manipulativeness. Proceeding with research projects without regard to the safety, privacy, or (informed) consent of research subjects, or sometimes the consent of the community to which they belong, is about being manipulative. In research terms, examples could include failing to inform someone that they are a research subject, misleading them in some way about the nature of their involvement, or revealing their confidences or identity without their consent.

There are extreme examples of manipulativeness, such as the Tuskegee syphilis scandal (see chapter 1), that have long exercised the policy-makers since the Nuremberg Trials. Despite attempts to legislate and regulate, cases of research subjects being abused or mistreated have continued to arise. While high-profile scandals are a sober reminder of the way researchers can mistreat and exploit vulnerable people, such extreme incidents of wrong-doing tend to overshadow more fine-grained and commonly occurring issues. A survey of conduct among more than 3,000 health science researchers discovered that over 7% of respondents admitted to having circumvented some minor aspect of normal requirements concerning the treatment of human subjects (Martinson et al., 2005). At root, manipulativeness is most likely to take place where there are inequalities of power between researchers and their subjects. As we have seen, quite often researchers may have more social, cultural, and symbolic capital (Bourdieu, 1988) than their research subjects. As academics, in addition to their educational qualifications, researchers are likely to have a position in a university or educational institution which can give them a higher social status in society than their research subjects. If a research project is funded by a prestigious body or research council this will tend to add further to the researcher's perceived social standing. Textbooks on interviewing, for example, often imply that the researcher is in a superior social position to that of the interviewee (Platt, 1981). Research involving children and teenagers, the taking of medical histories, or counselling relationships serve as examples of where there is a *prima facie* power imbalance between the researcher and the researched. It is very tempting for a researcher to take advantage of such a situation in gathering data.

There are, of course, situations where researchers may be interviewing their peers or those in more powerful social and economic positions than their own, but the majority of research subjects are likely to possess less social, cultural, and, perhaps, economic capital than the academic researcher. This realization should put us on our guard not to mislead or exploit research subjects, however inadvertently, in pursuing the answer to a research question or problem. For a social worker conducting research with vulnerable groups of people this is a particularly powerful obligation (see narrative 5.3).

Narrative 5.3

Interviewing the Vulnerable

I have worked on several research projects which involved interviewing often extremely vulnerable individuals. Several of the interviewees would

> seem to treat the interview almost as a counselling or therapy session, as an opportunity to talk about their problems in a confidential setting. Whilst mindful of the fact that I, as a researcher, am certainly not a trained counsellor I find it almost impossible in a situation where the interviewee has totally broken down to remain silent or impartial and not to offer at least some words of comfort.

This short narrative demonstrates that researchers can find it difficult not to be drawn into a relationship beyond that of "researcher" and "research subject." Views on where the dividing line should be drawn in this relationship depend, to some extent, on the attitude of the researcher to the research process. Where there is a belief that the role of the researcher is to be "neutral" or "detached" this is unlikely to support involvement with the concerns of the research subject beyond the strict confines of the project aims. Others, drawn from ethnographic research traditions, believe in forging close relationships in order to better understand the cultural milieu. The role of personality means that espoused methodological positions do not necessarily determine how relationships may be forged in practice.

Questions about the extent to which research is manipulative are tied to the concept of validity in research. To what extent can a piece of research be said to be accurate or true? Here, methodology which may be more likely to render a valid result may raise uncomfortable questions about the extent to which it is also manipulative or disrespectful toward research subjects. For example, research into the social phenomenon of football hooliganism has tended to deploy participant observation where researchers go "undercover." Sociologists often argue that this covert behavior is a necessary deception in order to understand the group in question, as revealing one's identity would alter the normal patterns of behavior among research subjects. Similar methods have been used by industrial sociologists, such as Hugh Beynon (1977) in studying the workplace.

Validity is also the key motivation for the use of a "control" or comparison group. Often research design, especially in biomedical investigation, involves the use of such a group which might be given a placebo rather than a new drug or treatment. Here, the use of the control group enables researchers to consider the extent to which results may be valid by comparison between the two groups, only one of which is actually receiving the new drug or treatment. However, some researchers question whether this conventional research design is in itself not manipulative. It may be argued that the members of the control group are disadvantaged as a result of being denied access to a treatment or innovation, such as a new curriculum for university students (Tolhurst, 2007).

Misunderstandings can easily occur in any social situation and this is also a risk in the research arena. Sometimes this can happen when research subjects form an impression that they will receive more than they actually receive on the basis of their co-operation. One of the challenges faced by all researchers is persuading potential participants to take part. Goodwill is often insufficient motivation to expect someone to willingly give up their time to complete a questionnaire or be interviewed. Solutions to this problem range from offering a copy of a published report or paper through to the chance to win a prize draw. Occasionally, though, there can be a temptation to make promises, either implicitly or explicitly, that the researcher cannot or later does not keep in the hope that the research subject will not subsequently pursue the matter or will forget about it. A classic example of this type of manipulativeness is failing to fulfill a promise to send a transcript of an interview to a research subject. While this is not, perhaps, the most serious transgression of the virtue of respectfulness it is more typical of a gentle slide from virtue to vice. Sometimes the failure, or at least the perception of the failure, to fulfill a promise to a research subject can have more serious consequences as illustrated in narrative 5.4.

Narrative 5.4

Permissions and Pressure

Not infrequently, research into aspects of the criminal law benefits from interviews with those who have been convicted and, occasionally, prisoners still serving a sentence. Access to lower security graded prisons is not too difficult and inmates are usually keen to speak to lawyers as they see them as another possibility of getting their cases aired either before the courts or the Criminal Cases Review Commission (CCRC). The reality that this was not going to happen is made clear in the first interview and most interviewees are content to continue.

Some years ago I had negotiated this sort of access both for myself and a younger researcher working with me. On one occasion this individual had gone alone to an open prison to do some follow-up interviews and had clearly left one inmate with the impression that his "fee" for being interviewed would be that we would put his case to the CCRC—something that could never have happened if only for the time it would have taken to investigate, even if we had had the facilities. To have investigated one story would have meant investigating all, and all had access to (in those days funded) legal representatives outside.

A letter duly arrived asking what progress was being made and this alerted me to the misunderstanding, so I replied explaining the position. He withdrew his co-operation in the research and, as he was seen as a leader amongst other prisoners, letters arrived from most of our interviewees doing the same, unless this particular individual's demands were complied with. I refused and the research ground to a halt. I was cross and frustrated and the body funding the research was keen that I give in to the demand to complete the work but it did not seem proper as this was not why I had approached any of the inmates in the first place.

As a footnote, some years later, after release, this individual did get his case before the CCRC, who rejected it in the same week as he received a 10-year sentence for a similar offence.

The narrative includes an indication of the uncomfortable situation researchers can find themselves in when the wishes of the research sponsor conflict with their own personal code of ethics. In this case, while the main investigator decided to suspend the project, the research-funding body took a more pragmatic view of the problem. This kind of conflict between the individual researcher and their research sponsor leads on to a consideration of a different vice which represents an excess, rather than a deficiency, of respectfulness.

PARTIALITY

While a lack of respectfulness can result in the researcher acting in a manipulative way, is it possible to have too much respectfulness? To make such a claim would, on the face of it, require some justification. However, in this respect there is a vice that I will label *partiality* which corresponds to an excess of respectfulness.

It is a moot question as to whether researchers can ever be completely "impartial." In most respected forms of academic research there is at least an expectation that an attempt will be made to minimize bias and to recognize where this might or has occurred. There are, though, distinct sets of assumptions that underpin the design and conduct of research. A positivist frame of reference holds that the researcher can remain independent of the phenomenon being scrutinized. This is a tradition more closely associated with the "hard" sciences where large data sets are used to test out hypotheses. Here, the researcher is seen as an impartial arbiter of the truth based on a dispassionate analysis of the observed "facts."

By contrast, the emphasis of a lot of research in the humanities and social sciences is on posing questions and generating theories rather than testing out propositions or formal hypotheses. Broadly speaking, this is an approach aimed at getting at the truth through inductive rather than deductive means. There are also varying perspectives about the nature of knowledge or epistemology. One highly influential point of view is that individuals socially construct their own version of reality rather than discovering "facts" (Berger & Luckmann, 1966). We are all, as individuals, shaped by our backgrounds and the cultures from which we come. Social constructivists believe that we reflect back these social and cultural assumptions when we seek to understand and interpret the world around us. Critical theorists also believe that truth is not value-free. They share a common commitment to radical social change and critiquing the social reality. Other theorists, sometimes labelled post-structuralists, contend that political power plays a significant role in the development of knowledge and that examining the "archae-ology" of knowledge claims reveals that there is no objective viewpoint (Foucault, 1972). These philosophical and sociological critiques, with regard to epistemology, mean that "truth telling" is, at best, a disputed concept.

For advocates of these alternative theories the researcher is not really an impartial technician but is themselves part of the research and cre-ative process. Many definitions of the research process found in popu-lar textbooks, though, tend to favor a positivist position and imply that researchers ought to be impartial. They suggest that research should be a systematic process with the purpose of getting to the "truth," estab-lishing "facts," and reaching conclusions. In other words, researchers should make every effort to avoid being "biased" or "partial." This is as much about reflective self-awareness of bias (see chapter 9) as it is about being without bias.

The vice of partiality refers to a very distinct form of bias. This is that shown towards the interests or concerns of powerful actors, such as sponsors or other influential third parties, at the expense of the pursuit of a line of enquiry based on an academic frame of reference, whether positivist or social constructivist. There is a long history of organiza-tions and policy-makers using research as a means of influencing and persuading others with respect to taking a particular course of action. In more recent years, the growth of biogenetics has resulted in a vast increase in corporate funding especially within research-based universities (Bok, 2003). It is significant to consider who defines the research problem. Is it the individual, academic researcher, or the organization (Merton 1973a)? If the definition of the research problem rests with the organization, the researcher may face added pressures that make partiality harder to resist.

Aside from seeking to use research evidence to justify a potentially predetermined course of action, an organizational sponsor may also use research as part of a delaying strategy, to excuse inaction (Merton 1973a). Arguably, this latter motivation has been present in attempts by the tobacco industry to use research in relation to passive smoking to ward off pressure for smoking to be banned in public places. According to a recent research study of scientists and technologists one in four reported that they had been asked to tailor their research results to suit the "preferred" outcome of a research sponsor (Prospect, 2006). There have also been cases where the financial sway of big pharmaceutical companies has been used to suppress the publication of research results which are not favorable to their interests when they are acting as a university sponsor (Kennedy, 1997). A large survey of health scientists found that more than 15% admitted to having altered aspects of the design, methodology, or results of a research study in response to pressure from a funding body or agency (Martinson et al., 2005). Thus, at the extreme, partiality may mean that the research findings of those supported by powerful organizations in the pharmaceutical and tobacco industries are unduly influenced by their sponsors' commercial interests (Barnes & Bero, 1998; Stelfox et al., 1998). In a study of academic papers about smoking, for example, those funded by the tobacco industry were much more likely to conclude that passive smoking was not harmful to health (Barnes & Bero, 1998). It is also claimed that corporate interests in the oil industry are now funding bogus scientific organizations that seek to discredit evidence with regard to climate change (Monbiot, 2006).

From a policy perspective the vice of partiality shares much in common with the "heresy" of "sponsorism" described as "the overprescription and control by government or other funding agencies of the form and content of research to the detriment of individual insight, creativity, even eccentricity" (Goodlad, 1995, 75). Governments have long been accused of putting "utilitarian" considerations before scientific significance with regard to research funding. In this respect, the German Nazi government of the 1930s was perhaps one of the first to systematically exploit scientific research capacity in this way (Merton, 1973b). In more recent times, the utility of academic investigation as a basis for policy-making has been expressed in terms of research that is "evidence-based." While this phrase was originally associated with medicine, expectations that the purpose and function of research is to provide an evidence-base for policy and practice are now common in other disciplines such as health, social care, and education (Clegg, 2007). Shaped by utilitarian considerations of what "works" in practice, these evidence-based agendas are seen by some critics as exercising a stranglehold over the academic community and stifling intellectual work (Blackmore, 2007; Clegg, 2007).

Partiality can clearly take many forms. I have highlighted sponsorism as a vice rather than taking a position that would prescribe particular methodological approaches as "partial." Matters of partiality may differ according to whether one believes that knowledge is "out there" waiting to be discovered or can only ever be understood as a constantly changing social phenomenon. A positivist might make an accusation of partiality against a social scientist who is following a research method based on the assumptions of social constructivism. The social scientist might retort that impartiality is really a methodological fiction, as the researcher's personality and beliefs always influence the research process.

Regardless of which of these research philosophies one may believe in there are times when individuals may become aware that partiality is operating. Certain research methods, such as participant observation, can raise this problem. In "insider research" a researcher draws heavily on their own engagement as a member of a community to switch between a "dual" identity as both a researcher and a colleague (see narrative 5.1). Here, the researcher can find it difficult not to become an overly sympathetic advocate on behalf of their colleagues rather than a more dispassionate analyst. Another example of where partiality can occur is in the following narrative (see narrative 5.5) where a researcher is aware that "likeability" is a factor which influences him in spending time with interviewees. This, he confesses, is partly shaped by whether the interviewee is "a personable woman" rather than "an ugly old male." One reaction to this narrative might be that the interviewer is not a fit person to be conducting research. Another might be that acknowledging one's own biases, rather than burying them deep in the sub-conscious, is the first step toward becoming a better researcher.

Narrative 5.5

The Ethics of Attraction

In one form or another qualitative research is often about meeting people and interviewing them. Formally, informally, structured or unstructured it forms a key to much work. One of the problems I have— and I can't imagine I'm the only one—is that my attitude, behavior, and demeanor in interview situations can vary according to how much I *like* someone.

It is something I have to constantly watch and monitor and it can pervade all aspects of the situation. If I really like someone I might be "easier" in the interview than with someone I dislike who I might "press," I might spend longer with someone who is amenable and pleasant than with someone who is disagreeable. I have to be honest enough to say that these difficulties can be particularly marked in interviews with the opposite gender—I'd much rather spend an hour chatting with a personable woman than an hour with an ugly old male! This represents real problems with the integrity of the research product—after all, who is likeable and who is not is a very subjective assessment made on fairly dubious grounds by me—with all my prejudices and white middle-class male baggage.

I take comfort from the fact that I am aware of this "bias to the nice" but it does raise some interesting ethical and methodological issues.

CONCLUSION

Respectfulness toward research subjects is a virtue which is widely cited as integral to any form of research which purports to be conducted in an "ethical" manner. However, it is a virtue which needs to be lived out, in all its complexities, rather than idly asserted as a mantra. Researchers have learnt to habitually stress the importance of treating research subjects "with respect" as part of the rules of the game in obtaining permission to proceed with a research project or in making applications for funding. What is important is that the complexities of fulfilling such an intention need to be thought through. To do this demands an awareness of the risks of manipulativeness and partiality. The most common challenges researchers face in this regard is guarding against complacency or idleness that can result in research subjects feeling that they have been taken for granted or "used." Failing to fulfill promises to provide research subjects with meaningful follow-up information on the results of a study or carelessness in holding confidential information is more commonly linked to such attitudes rather than the more extreme cases of abuse or mistreatment that tend to grab the headlines.

6

RESOLUTENESS

It's a disaster. Nothing went as I'd planned. I'm not even sure if the whole premise of my thesis will stand up. I may have to trash the whole thing. (Straker & Hall, 1999, 419)

INTRODUCTION

Resoluteness is an essential moral virtue for researchers in all fields of enquiry. Those who do not possess it will rarely achieve much of lasting worth. The research process can be demanding and arduous, lasting several years and, in some respects, the length of an academic career. Significant scientific and academic figures from the past are often associated with career-long struggles to make "breakthroughs" or gain wider recognition for the nature of their research. For example, it is estimated that between 1856 and 1863 Gregor Mendel, an Augustinian monk, tested 28,000 pea plants in experiments that led to his discovery of the basic laws of inheritance. His painstaking cross-breeding pro-gram resulted in the law of segregation and discovered how genes are passed on through the generations. While Mendel's work was largely unrecognized in his lifetime he is now often cited as the father of modern genetics. In many respects, Thomas Edison, the American inventor, lies at the opposite end of the spectrum to Mendel. Edison was famous in his lifetime with a string of inventions and innovations to his name including the electric light bulb and the phonograph. He was also commercially astute, taking out over a thousand patents. However, in common with Mendel, Edison was a workaholic who reportedly tested over a thousand materials before discovering one suitable for a light bulb. Fittingly, Edison was attributed with the oft-quoted remark that genius is one percent inspiration and 99% perspiration.

There are dangers, of course, of mythologizing the "greatness" of researchers from the past. The legends associated with Mendel and Edison are, like with many other figures in the history of science and discovery, disputed (Judson, 2004). However, in thinking of the research process itself as a long and arduous "journey" it is instructive to reflect on these lessons of history (Brew 2001b). At times, this journey can be slow, unproductive, dispiriting, and lonely, especially when results are disappointing or the search for inspiration proves illusive. This chapter will consider the importance of resoluteness as a moral virtue and the risks when this virtue lapses. While this is explored mainly in relation to the stage at which researchers seek to generate data, ideas, or other materials in relation to their research, resoluteness is a virtue that is relevant at all stages of investigation.

UNBENDING INTENT

Research, regardless of discipline or field of study, requires a degree of *resoluteness* in order to generate research data, ideas, or concepts. This requires individuals to be purposeful and determined and not to give up when the going gets tough. According to Thomas Aquinas, moral virtues are dispositions that help us determine what we want to achieve. It is necessary to possess (or at least develop) resoluteness in order to achieve something. In parallel with resoluteness, Aquinas identified fortitude as one of his four, so-called "cardinal" virtues. As a virtue, resoluteness is very different in nature from respectfulness, the focus of discussion in the previous chapter. Respectfulness is essentially, in Pincoffs' (1986) terms, a non-instrumental virtue whereas resoluteness requires action. It requires a determination to achieve a particular deed.

Having resilience and an "unbending intent" (Brew 2001a) is vital if researchers are to succeed in generating data, results, findings, concepts, or artefacts of some description. Brew explains the meaning of "unbending intent" by reference to taking on rather than shirking challenges. A research project, even those to which funding might be attached, can be an arduous labour of love which can lead to researchers falling out of love with the object of their fascination at frequent intervals. Researchers meet many obstacles during the course of their work: a lack of funding, rejected proposals and papers, uncooperative interviewees, a poor response rate from survey instruments, missing books from libraries, a lack of inspiration, or simply boredom. More fundamentally, researchers may find that their original preconceptions or hypotheses, often based to some extent on their beliefs or values, are challenged or even contradicted by their own results. Determination to persist in a research endeavor is a critical virtue if these types of obstacles are to be overcome. While research makes considerable intellectual demands it also requires the will to achieve.

All academic investigation demands patience, particularly in the collection of data. Arguably, more patience is required in some disciplines than in others. This is illustrated by different rates of publication across the disciplines (Moed, 2005). The reason for this is related both to established differences in the culture and working practices of different academic disciplines and to the length of time it takes in some fields to obtain accurate and reliable results which need to be rigorously tested before reporting or publication can take place (Becher & Trowler, 2001; Moed, 2005). While pressure has grown for academics to publish their research findings more quickly in response to audit and funding allocation (see chapter 10), there is still a need for lengthy and detailed data collection and analysis processes to be completed (see narratives 6.1 and 6.2).

Narrative 6.1

Repeating the Experiment

To accomplish good research can take a very long time. To get a good, reliable result can take us anything up to seven years just to get one decent paper. This is a long time to perform experiments and to do that the graduate students need patience. We all need patience. In the seven years we will probably repeat the same experiment at least three times. I request that the same experiment is performed at least three times as we need the same result from the experiment to confirm the data. So it can be very frustrating especially for young graduate students who need to publish for the benefit of their career. So we have to persuade them not to jump to conclusions. You need patience to be a scientist.

Narrative 6.2

Slow Progress

Archeologists have to be incredibly patient. Excavation work can be slow and unproductive. Working in a place like Egypt is also very hot and tiring. In the evenings it can be lonely and there is not much to do. It can take weeks and weeks and the only thing you may have to show for it is a

> tiny fragment. All the fragments are important though in understanding the whole story. Despite what people might think, you don't suddenly find a whole new town or city. It's not glamorous work. Sometimes you don't find anything and even after you find something you need a lot of patience in figuring out its importance.

Researchers also need determination after completing data collection and analysis, particularly in the "writing up" phase of research. Writing demands a different skill set to data collection and can be a challenging task even for the most seasoned researcher writing in their native language. The writing up of research is frequently just the beginning of a process of rewriting a thesis, paper, or report that can stretch into months and even years of amendments. Peer-reviewing processes deployed by most academic journals demand patience and a preparedness to amend in response to criticism. The negative nature of some of this feedback can test the resoluteness of the researcher to the limit.

Studying for a postgraduate research degree, such as a PhD, is the conventional way in which many trainee academics first encounter a major research project. A doctoral degree normally requires the production of a thesis anywhere between 20,000 words, for a professional doctorate or doctorate by publication, to as much as 120,000 words for a conventional PhD. The growth of professional doctorates in areas such as management, nursing, midwifery, and education allows participants to focus on connecting professional experience with "problems of relevance" (Gordon, 2005, 41) to that community. Professional doctorates provide research students with a stronger framework of support, typically including taught elements, continuous assessment, and a peer group cohort. Both conventional and professional doctorates involve the production of an extended piece of research that can take many years to complete. High attrition rates testify to the challenges associated with completing the thesis. It is an understandably daunting prospect especially for those with little or no prior experience of undertaking an extended piece of academic research.

In recent years universities have come under closer scrutiny and increased pressure to improve completion performance to justify continued public funding. In 1997 the attrition rate for Australian postgraduate research students was 34%, notably higher than that for undergraduate students (Kiley & Mullins, 2005). A study of attrition for doctoral study in the United States demonstrated that rates varied substantially between disciplines and universities from as few as 19% of students dropping out of a Chemistry PhD at a rural university to as many as 76% failing to complete an English doctorate at an urban institution (Lovitts, 2001). In a UK context there is increasing concern about doctoral completion, leading to pressure from research councils for improvements in success rates (Gordon, 2005).

A range of academic, financial, and social factors test the resoluteness of doctoral students. According to a report from the English funding council, the student most likely to complete will be those who are young, from overseas, in receipt of funding, and studying for a doctorate in the natural sciences on a full-time basis (HEFCE, 2005). These factors relate closely to the very different levels of completion across the disciplines. Younger, full-time students tend to take doctorates in the natural sciences where completion rates are higher. PhD students in the arts, humanities, and social sciences, where lower rates of completion prevail, are much more likely to be older and registered on a part-time basis. The statistics reveal starkly different chances of completion between those studying in part-time and full-time mode. In the UK, just 34% of students who start a PhD on a part-time basis complete within seven years whilst the figure for full-time students is 71% (HEFCE, 2005).

However, in understanding why the majority persist, and ultimately succeed, it is perhaps more instructive to consider what motivates so many researchers. It would be a mistake to assume that the archetypical doctoral research student is necessarily young and inexperienced, in the same way as the profile of university undergraduate students has altered radically as a result of the expansion of the modern higher education system. The contemporary doctoral student is more typically a mature individual with either prior or current experience in a professional career context. In England, 65% of students are at least 25 years old when they begin a doctoral programme (HEFCE, 2005).

MOTIVATION TO SUCCEED

In considering what motivates students to undertake a doctoral research a useful starting point is the distinction between intrinsic and extrinsic motivation. Intrinsic motivation refers to the desire to do something for its own sake because you find the particular activity inherently satisfying. Extrinsic motivation, by contrast, is about engaging in an activity as an instrument for gaining recognition, reward, or, perhaps, more negatively, to avoid punishment. The motivation of those registered for professional doctorates has been divided into three "types" based on the essential distinction between intrinsic and extrinsic motivation (Scott at al., 2004). Those extrinsically motivated either see a doctorate as part of their professional initiation and important to career development (type 1) or part of their continued development as experienced professionals (type 2). However, a sense of personal fulfilment and pursuing research based on personal curiosity is of more importance to those who are intrinsically motivated (type 3) (Scott, et al., 2004). Curiosity is an essential predisposition or intellectual virtue for any researcher. Despite the fact that doctoral students are increasingly drawn from mid-career professional contexts they are strongly motivated by type 3 intrinsic interest. This also indicates a desire among researchers for intellectual and emotional growth as learners (Leonard et al., 2005). They regard a doctorate as an ultimate personal challenge to "prove myself at the higher level" (p135). This runs counter to the prevailing emphasis at a policy level on the extrinsic, employment-related benefits of higher degree study and the allied assumption that doctoral students are pre-career, immature learners (Quality Assurance Agency for higher education, 2004).

Another of the primary obstacles faced by researchers is getting funded. Here, power relations play an important role. In this respect, it would be a mistake to imagine that every academic researcher is necessarily undertaking a project which matches their own intellectual orientation. In a survey of over 650 academics it was found that one in five do not pursue research which is of personal interest to them while around 40% align their research area with available funding opportunities (Macfarlane & Cheng, 2008). The priorities of research centers, government, private sector, and other charitable bodies dictate what types of research project will gain financial support. The themes which may be favoured by such bodies do not necessarily coincide with the personal research agenda of the individual researcher. The power rests with the funding body rather than the individual. This makes it particularly difficult for academics, especially in certain science fields requiring expensive equipment and extensive laboratory-based or clinical trials, to pursue personal priorities. Research themes, topics, and even methodologies can go in and out of fashion during an academic career. It takes both courage (see chapter 4) and resolution for researchers to stick with areas of research work that fall out of favor or fashion and for which, as a consequence, there may be limited private or public funding support available. This takes an act of faith and a resolute spirit.

Power relations can also have a significant effect on students registered for a doctoral research degree. The inequality in power relations between supervisor and supervisee, the supervisor's own research interests, and the focus of funding for projects under their control are all factors likely to play a substantial role in determining the direction of the student's thesis. This may be helpful for some individuals in maturing their own ideas but might be experienced as disempowering by others with more clearly formulated research agendas (Salmon, 1994).

Statistics from leading research councils show that a larger percentage of doctoral theses are now completed within the expected and funded time-frame. Less than three-quarters of theses funded by the UK Economic and Social Research Council were completed within four years in 1990. By 2002 this figure had risen to four-fifths (Economic and Social Research Council, 2007). The relatively recent improvement in completion rates for doctoral degrees is related, at least in part, to supervisors encouraging students to pursue more closely defined and circumscribed projects. This contrasts with a tradition, especially strong in the arts and humanities, where students define their own topic or question. While better completion rates are a positive sign in some respects, this trend has been linked to the need for supervisors to meet the demands of externally funded projects where the identification of topics needs to be of more immediate relevance to industry rather than to the discipline (Neumann, 2007).

A battle of wills can take place when a research student wants to tackle a question or topic that a supervisor deems not to be feasible within the time-frame of a doctoral study. The push for timely completion is associated with a scaling back of the scope of the doctoral thesis on pragmatic rather than intellectual grounds. "Do-able" topics are replacing more risky ones and there is a tendency to discriminate against part-time students who understandably take longer on average to complete (Neumann, 2007). These trends represent a pragmatic reaction to an increased expectation that growing numbers of doctoral students will complete on time. However, they raise important concerns about the extent to which the research student has "ownership" of their own topic.

FRIENDS AND FAMILY

While supportive and constructive criticism can help to motivate a research student, a lack of interest and attention or purely negative feedback can have the reverse effect. Researchers need as much help as they can get in seeing through their projects to completion. Like any other learner, they often depend on the support of peers, family members, and friends who can play a significant role in providing both emotional support and intellectual guidance. Any cursory examination of the acknowldgements sections of theses reveals the importance of such sources of support. Some researchers, particularly in the arts, humanities, and social sciences, regard research subjects or participants as co-workers in the process of intellectual understanding and will often acknowledge their support too.

Finally, and perhaps most significantly, research is an activity that is often fitted in around a range of other social, family, and work-related commitments both for academic staff and research students alike. It is an activity that demands sacrificing time and energy for an uncertain outcome. Despite the prior professional and life experience that mature students bring to research study, they are faced with other, more significant challenges. In Leonard, et al.'s (2005) study, half of their respondents had children living at home. They regarded their PhD studies as something that they had to fit around their children rather than the other way round. Many academic staff are expected to undertake research as part of their terms of employment. Others may feel impelled to do so as part of their identity as academics (see chapter 12). However, this will typically form only part of a workload that will include other time-consuming duties such as teaching, management, administration, and service commitments. Sustaining commitment to pursuing a research project is a considerable practical undertaking and, in effect, a life-style choice. It will test the resolution of the individual to pursue their goals despite the temptations of cutting corners to achieve their aims or the dangers of becoming entrenched in unproductive modes of thinking or styles of investigation.

LAZINESS

The obstacles and personal challenges connected with gathering data and the development of ideas can sap the will of the researcher. The vice of laziness is sometimes bred by boredom or frustration with the pace of progress or the extent to which research is producing the anticipated outcomes. Frustrations can occur at any stage of the research process but are often most associated with setbacks in research design or data collection.

In data collection, methods deployed can prove disappointing in yielding meaningful results, sometimes as a result of insufficient planning or piloting. Poor rates of return can prove frustrating for those relying on the completion of questionnaires. Interviewees can be uncooperative or simply unavailable. Experiments can fail to produce the anticipated results. Such setbacks are an integral part of the reality of research but can also be the starting point for laziness. An example might include compromising on the planned extent of data collection by cutting back on the scope or ambition of a project. It might simply mean deciding not to bother to send out reminders to members of a sample who have yet to return a questionnaire or cutting back on the planned number of interviews. Another example of laziness is to rework old data. This involves using data collected from a previous piece of research to bolster the perceived extent of research in a new study. While many researchers find it necessary to compromise on their original good intentions there comes a point when laziness in collecting data can lead on to further temptations to deceive others about the extent to which goals have been achieved (see chapter 7).

Laziness can occur at later stages in the research process through using the same data to write several academic papers for publication. This is sometimes referred to as "recycling." This is a practice which is associated with attempts by researchers to artificially boost perceptions of their research productivity in connection with "performative" expectations (see chapter 10). There are circumstances though where such behavior may be justifiable. A researcher may legitimately write papers based on the same work for different audiences, such as academic peers, colleagues in an applied field or profession, and the broader public. Another facet of laziness is the "salami-slicing" of data. Here, a data set that might be more appropriately presented in a single academic publication is presented as a series of papers to increase the appearance of individual research productivity. It can lead to publication of academic papers based on insubstantial research data rather than a more detailed, perhaps longitudinal study. There are potentially negative implications of this vice for the wider academic community, as premature publication or publication based on insubstantial data can lead to misleading or poorly supported conclusions. The prevalence of this type of behavior in relation to publication has also been associated with pressures on academic staff to demonstrate their productivity in relation to quality audit of research in universities (see chapter 10).

Laziness may take more subtle forms. The challenges associated with research design and methodology can lead to researchers becoming over-reliant on a particular form of investigation or technique, such as the use of survey instruments or interviews. They can easily become entrenched in a "comfort zone" connected with familiar methods of data collection and analysis or theoretical frameworks. Sometimes these tried and trusted techniques will be inappropriate in tackling a particular research problem or question. The researcher will then be confronted by the challenge of whether they are prepared to try something different and use an unfamiliar investigatory style or tool. This demands the associated virtue of courage (see chapter 4).

INFLEXIBILITY

At the other extreme, a researcher may become so resolute that they are insufficiently flexible in their approach to the research idea, problem, or question at hand. This behavior can manifest itself in the vice of *inflexibility*. Research is rarely an uncomplicated, linear process that moves seamlessly from proposal to conclusion. Along the way there are disappointments and things that do not work to plan. Often the research design may prove a disappointment for a number of reasons. A methodology considered at the outset to be well suited may later prove unsuitable. An experiment repeated without success or relevant insight into the problem or question at hand needs to be reconsidered. Hypotheses can be rapidly displaced by alternative propositions as the research progresses. Yet, there comes a point when every researcher has to call a temporary halt at least to data collection or reading the (possibly, vast) literature in order to move their research project forward. While coming to "premature conclusions" is a risk, so is never reaching any kind of conclusion. In his classic work *The Sociological Imagination*, C. Wright Mills quotes the following passage in encouraging academics to share their thinking thus far:

> The constant warning against premature conclusions and foggy generalities implies, unless properly qualified, a possible taboo against all thinking. If ever thought has to be held in abeyance until it has been completely corroborated, no basic approach seems possible and we limit ourselves to the level of mere symptoms. (Max Horkheimer quoted by Mills, 1970, 137)

A researcher needs to guard against inflexibility if they are not to get bogged down and be unable to move to the stage at which they can give voice to their own contribution. Here, it is important to consider the way that reflexivity (see chapter 9) can act as a guard against this vice. Dogmatic persistence is not always the best option and researchers need to be prepared to exercise some flexibility.

Inflexibility can have an emotional as well as a practical dimension. Here, researchers must face the possibility that the results of research may challenge their own cherished assumptions, sometimes formally expressed as a hypothesis. Straker and Hall (1999, 419) write about their own experiences of "crisis and cognitive dissonance" when the results of research contradicted their own personal beliefs and values.

One of the researchers, Alison Straker, was a keen proponent of the so-called "contact hypothesis," that close and sustained contact between different racial and ethnic groups will lead to improved understanding and attitudes (Powers & Ellison, 1995). However, her research observations started to show opposite indications to that of the hypothesis. Rather than demonstrating positive outcomes, the international exchanges which formed the focus for her research project showed they could create negative experiences for participants "as evidence amassed before my eyes to suggest that frequently face-to-face contacts, however positive, do little to affect opinions about groups as a whole" (Straker & Hall, 1999, 428).

Even a "negative" outcome is of interest and, in fact, may help to break more fresh ground than simply confirming an established theory or hypothesis. While Straker experienced "feelings of loss and discomfort" (Straker & Hall, 1999, 429) stemming from her research findings, her supervisor saw her results as an interesting opportunity for her to say something different. Straker was able to recover her thesis, capitalizing on the unexpected outcome of her research and seeking to explain why, in the context of a post-industrial society, the contact hypothesis may be of limited significance. In many respects, being sufficiently open or reflexive is an essential part of being an academic researcher (see chapter 9). Experiencing discomfort rather than comfort mirrors the notion of criticism, a distinctive characteristic of a "higher" education (Barnett, 1990).

While the example refers to someone who might, broadly, be defined as a social scientist, possessing ideological or theoretical commitments which might be challenged as a result of one's own research endeavors is not an uncommon scenario. Researchers from all fields are motivated to engage in academic investigation through a desire to develop work that will conform with or lend support to their own view of the world. In Alison Straker's case this was, essentially, one based on liberal humanism but other researchers are equally committed to other value sets and "world views." The "scientist" has a public image as a detached and cautious expert but this does not mean that the conduct of scientific research is necessarily "value-neutral" (Fuller, 2006, 57).

CONCLUSION

Resoluteness demands more than the strength of character to press on when results are disappointing. It also requires the emotional flexibility to allow the evidence or the "data" to tell its own story rather than expecting results to follow a predictable, and perhaps more desirable pattern. This requires the researcher to be versatile or chameleon-like. Hence, resoluteness means much more than simply carrying on regardless. It implies a determination to unveil the truth, however confirming or disconfirming to one's view of the world this may be. The importance of pursuing the truth and recognizing one's own fallibility in this process is another central virtue in research which will form the basis of the next chapter.

7

SINCERITY

The whole fabric of research is trust. (Elizabeth Neufeld, quoted in Hardwig, 1991, 693)

INTRODUCTION

At heart, research is concerned with the pursuit of truth. We expect researchers to be committed to this struggle, whether we believe "truth" to be objectively observable or socially constructed. While researchers must possess basic skills that enable them to pursue their scholarly interests, at a moral level what matters most is that researchers are committed to do their best in getting at the truth. This demands the moral virtue of *sincerity*.

This chapter will consider the importance of this virtue mainly in the context of the "creation" of research. This phase of the research process refers to the conversion of data, materials, and other fruits of the researcher's efforts into the production of "results." These might take the form of findings, theorems, concepts, models, critiques, compositions, or artefacts. This is a difficult and demanding process involving decisions about how to represent the results of academic labour. It means, invariably, entering into a process of selection and interpretation regardless of whether one's approach relies on quantitative or qualitative techniques. All researchers must use their judgment to discriminate in favor of certain forms of data analysis or interpretation and against or in preference to other available techniques or tests. Here, what is vital is that such endeavors are authentic representations of what the researcher has found out or, at least, *believes* to be true. This is the essence of sincerity.

This chapter will identify why academics are under a particular obligation in respect of this virtue, an obligation connected both to their position as public servants and the historic privileges of academic freedom. It will examine the components of truthfulness and consider the effect of both private and public failure to live up to the demands of sincerity and the trust vested in academics by society.

A POSITION OF TRUST

Despite the growing privatization and commercialization of the modern university, many academics continue to work for publicly funded institutions of higher education. This gives them both a status and a responsibility as public servants. Part of this responsibility is to fulfill the expectation that they will act in the public interest by pursuing, and reporting, the truth as far as they are able. Academics are, in the words of Williams (2002), in a position of trust. Their obligations as public servants are complicated by the increasing dependence of university research on private sources of funding. However, for research to be seen as "credible," the involvement of academics is still a critical component, at least as far as policy-makers are concerned (Williams & Robinson, 2007).

The obligation of researchers to pursue the truth is also interrelated with the Humboldtian idea of the university. Wilhelm von Humboldt, the founder of the University of Berlin, believed that it was in the best interests of the state to allow research and intellectual activity to go on within universities without interference. He argued that universities ought to be sanctuaries for intellectuals and that the "fruitfulness" of this unfettered activity would, ultimately, prove to be of greater benefit for the state than would be achieved through an interventionist policy (von Humboldt, 1970). Reinforcing the Humboldtian vision, Weber contends that the only "virtue" which universities should be required to inculcate is "intellectual integrity" involving "a relentless clarity about themselves" (Weber, 1973a, 21). In other words, in return for the independence and privilege of academic status, complete honesty or integrity is essential. This is part of the implied compact between universities and society. This Humboldtian vision of academic freedom is deeply embedded in the psyche of modern higher education despite an increasingly interventionist state.

THE GILLIGAN AFFAIR

According to the philosopher Bernard Williams (2002) truthfulness consists of two virtues that he refers to as accuracy and sincerity. In extracting this double meaning, Williams draws on *Wahrhaftigkeit*, the German word for truthfulness. It is not difficult to see why accuracy is so important in research. It manifests itself in various ways during the course of the research process through activities such as recording the results of research, the notes from an interview, or references from a literature search. Without accuracy research is rendered unreliable and the reputation of the researcher is also damaged in the process. Another consequence is that an erosion of trust may occur, both within the discipline and among the public, which will adversely affect other researchers and their associated institutions. A good illustration of how trust can be damaged by claims of inaccuracy is provided by the so-called Gilligan affair.

On September 24, 2002 the British Prime Minister Tony Blair stated that "extensive, detailed and authoritative" intelligence had concluded that Iraq had chemical and biological weapons which "could be activated within 45 minutes" (Blair, 2002). This statement was later seen to be highly influential in the train of events that led to the decision of Britain, the United States, and other allies to invade Iraq and depose the country's president Saddam Hussein. In May 2003 a BBC (British Broadcasting Corporation) journalist called Andrew Gilligan made a live radio broadcast reporting that an unnamed source had stated that the government had probably known that the 45 minutes claim was "wrong" or "questionable." The unnamed source was later revealed as Dr David Kelly, a British government scientist and biological weapons expert, who subsequently committed suicide after his identity was revealed to the media by the government. However, a later BBC enquiry, headed by Ronald Neil, concluded that Gilligan's notes were insufficiently detailed to support his allegation regarding Prime Minister Blair's so-called 45-minute warning. The Neil Report also identified five journalistic values: truth and accuracy, serving the public interest, impartiality and diversity of opinion, independence, and accountability (British Broadcasting Corporation, 2004).

There is a clear link between these journalistic values and the ones we would associate with academic research. In other words, they might equally be applied to any academic researcher. While Andrew Gilligan was a journalist rather than an academic researcher this affair should resonate with all those concerned with research. As a fellow journalist, Andrew Marr asks how many colleagues within his own profession would be capable of backing up their own stories with detailed and accurate notes (Marr, 2004). As academics, many of us are rarely (if ever) called upon to produce the detailed notes or raw data that justify the conclusions we have reached. While it is true that codes of research conduct often require research data to be retained for at least five years, or up to 20 years in respect to clinical trials of new drugs, how many of us, if asked to do so, would be confident that our data, or interpretations of conversations, would stand up to such intense scrutiny?

Being capable of meeting this kind of challenge, though, is at least in theory common to researchers and journalists in making claims to truth. The "reproducibility" of research results is all important in scientific experiments and the reputation of academics in fields, such as chemistry, can be destroyed when published data is not deemed to be reproducible by other respected scientists. This is why a scientist with integrity will often perform the same experiment many times before being satisfied that the results are accurate. Unlike researchers in the humanities and social sciences, academics in the natural sciences tend to work in large teams and need to be able to trust their co-researchers, including their graduate students who are normally an integral part of research work. The leader of a research team will often ask to see proof of experiments undertaken but the extent to which they can check all the procedures used in producing data can be limited by practical considerations of time and resources.

There are other parallels between the Andrew Gilligan affair and trust in research. When an academic asserts something on the basis of "research" they are trading off public trust in them and the institutions, such as universities or learned research bodies, to which they belong. Similarly, the BBC, as a respected and well-established organization of international standing, trades off its reputation for accuracy and truthfulness when it broadcasts (British Broadcasting Corporation, 2004). This means that when the BBC broadcasts or academics speak, people largely believe what is said.

A HIGHER STANDARD OF TRUTH

Researchers are expected to be truthful beyond the standards that might be applied to certain other professions, such as politicians. The convention of British politics is that government ministers may answer questions and make statements in such a way that they tell less than the whole truth. This allows them to be selective in what they say, omit information if they choose, and give, in the process, a potentially misleading impression (Williams 2002). In the words of the former top British civil servant Sir Robert Armstrong, who was Secretary to the British Cabinet during the 1980s, it is about being "economical with the truth" (Kleinedler et al., 2005, 34). Armstrong's phrase is a tongue-in-cheek way of distinguishing between lying and misleading people through omission of certain facts. This is a lower standard of behavior in relation to truth-telling than is normally expected of an academic researcher. Such individuals are expected to make a full rather than partial disclosure.

In legal terms, a parallel might be drawn with the English legal principles of *caveat emptor* ("let the buyer beware") and *uberrima fide* ("complete or utmost good faith"). In most contractual agreements the former principle applies, meaning that the seller of goods or services does not need to disclose anything which might have a negative bearing on a potential sale unless explicitly asked a direct question. However, in some contractual situations, such as an insurance agreement, the latter principle of *uberrima fide* applies. This demands a much higher standard of honesty whereby all pertinent facts must be disclosed by a potential seller even if the buyer does not ask for the information. This parallel is instructive in understanding why accounts of methodology in research normally contain some detailed caveats about weaknesses and limitations. The "good" researcher is open about the extent to which he or she believes that they have succeeded in their own objectives. They enter into a discourse of self-criticism and communicate on the basis of full rather than partial disclosure.

What is sometimes referred to as the acts and omissions doctrine (Glover, 1977) has other implications for a researcher than might generally apply if following the norms of behavior in society. These norms would dictate that in some circumstances it is morally "less bad" to omit to act than to act. For example, in debates about euthanasia it is often asserted that there is a moral difference between allowing someone with a terminal illness to die by not giving them drugs to help them stay alive longer as opposed to acting in some positive way to, in effect, "kill" the person more quickly by administering an overdose of painkilling drugs. This reasoning is subject to the criticism that omitting to do something can be just as immoral as doing something. A researcher might lie or fabricate results. These are acts which are clearly wrong. They might also, however, choose to ignore carrying out certain tests which they know will probably contradict a result or choose to ignore other information which casts doubt on their thesis or previous publications. These are omissions to act. Are these omissions any less wrong?

Here, it can be argued that the result of both acts and omissions are essentially the same: the wider academic community and, perhaps, society more generally is deliberately misled. Hence, if the result of an omission can be foreseen it is harder to argue that there is a substantive moral difference between an act and an omission. The key difference, in relation to research, is between false statements made in error and false statements made with intent. In a well-known passage from *Gaudy Night,* a mystery novel about an Oxford women's college by Dorothy L. Sayers originally published in 1935, one of the principal characters makes the following statement in respect to a discussion about academic integrity:

> The only ethical principle which has made science possible is that the truth must be told all the time. If we do not penalise false statements made in error then we open up the way for false statements made by intent, and the false statement made by intent is the most serious crime that a scientist can commit. (Sayers, 2003, 413)

Hence, while any false statement is to be regretted, a false statement made with intent is the most reprehensible since there is an intention to deceive. This does not imply that false statements made in error are not matters of considerable regret but that the extent to which the researcher is acting with sincerity is the key to understanding the difference. Indeed, an excessive fear of being accused of deception through seeking to publish results of research in good faith may ultimately damage the pursuit of truth in science.

The Gilligan affair focuses on matters of trust and accuracy in reporting the results of research. However, it is also about sincerity. In many ways, sincerity is a better word than truthfulness inasmuch as the researcher may not be, or may subsequently be shown not to be, accurate when making a statement or reporting other results of research. Indeed, for academics truth is always something "tentative" and error can merely be "outdated truth" (Ashby, 1967, 46). Truth, from an academic perspective, is not only temporary but may often be subjective. New "truths" can emerge as a result of research which uses different methods, takes place at different times in history or in a different cultural milieu. Historians, for example, often rely on the availability of documentary evidence which may be suppressed or withheld for personal or political reasons. When such documents are made public they can cast an entirely new light on historical incidents and lead to reinterpretations of events. However, a sincere researcher is endeavoring to the best of their abilities to be truthful or authentic in their work at the time at which they are engaged with it. Being sincere implies doing one's best to be accurate both in reporting research results and to oneself. The caveats and disclaimers are as important as the claims to truth one might make. It is about a "disposition to make sure that one's assertion expresses what one actually believes" (Williams, 2002, 96). Hence, this is a truthfulness better conveyed, perhaps, by the German word *Wahrhaftigkeit* incorporating both sincerity and accuracy (Williams 2002). Without sincerity the whole credibility of the research process would be called into question.

In the history of academic research there have been many infamous incidents that have come into the public domain illustrating transgressions of this virtue. In recent times the case of Korean scientist Woo Suk Hwang is perhaps one of the best known. Professor Hwang was hailed as a national hero in Korea after reporting that he had successfully cloned an Afghan dog in a major breakthrough for stem cell research. It later transpired that Professor Hwang had fabricated his research findings (Henderson & Salmon, 2005). Like other researchers, Professor Hwang was subject to the "traditional rules" of research, one of which is that researchers should make an original contribution to their field (Brew, 2001a). This expectation builds a pressure to come up with something that is "original." Such an expectation is not confined to just high-profile researchers. It also applies to the tens of thousands who are pursuing a research project as part of a postgraduate research degree or are otherwise unlikely to attract widespread public attention beyond the narrow confines of a small academic community. The use of phrases such as "original contribution" and "significant contribution" characterizes the requirements of doctoral degrees across national contexts (Noble, 1994). This is quite a daunting requirement for an inexperienced researcher. It is thus, perhaps understandable, if not excusable, that some are tempted to falsify their results in an attempt to satisfy such a high expectation.

Occasionally, scientists and other academics are forced to make embarrassing admissions of error due to inaccuracies or inconsistencies in their own research methods. In 2004, Dr David Ho, a molecular biologist and leading AIDS researcher, retracted a finding reported in a paper published with others in *Science* that he had found a key antiviral factor that helped to explain why some people who contract HIV still manage to survive long-term. The retraction stated that the antiviral factor did not, in fact, come from the white blood cells of HIV-infected patients and was due to a laboratory error (Zhang et al., 2004). The key to ensuring that scientific researchers do not have to make such retractions is reproducibility. An honest scientist will repeat the same experiment many times in order to ensure reproducibility. Rushing to make claims through publication in the natural sciences is a dangerous course of action.

The nature of research is cumulative. Researchers rely heavily on building on the ideas and theories of others and, to some extent, have to take what they say on trust. This is partly because of the fragmentation of knowledge which means that few modern academics, if any, could claim complete mastery in all cognate areas of relevance to their field (Hardwig, 1991). In mathematics it might take many months, years, or even centuries to be able to fully test out a mathematical "proof." The academic careers of mathematicians are often based on building on or filling in the gaps of theorems. Therefore, a high degree of trust is necessary in the accuracy and sincerity of the work of other scholars, as illustrated in narrative 7.1.

Narrative 7.1

Trusting the Proof

As a mathematician, I get recognition for formulating the problem in a precise way or posing new problems. When I want to communicate what I have found then there are some ethical questions. Our training (as mathematicians) is how to put our thoughts down in a mathematical form and using propositional logic to prove things. It's not like doing an experiment and trying to sort out the mess and seeing patterns that other people don't see. Mathematics progresses by defining new concepts and solving problems. It is essential to learn how to distinguish what I know (what I have proof of) from what I expect. It is not necessary to have proofs for everything, just to know the difference. In a way, it's like building a house. It is not necessary for me to make everything from scratch. I can buy bricks from a friend, for example, trusting him. But if the house collapses I need to know where the problem could be. Is it the way that I designed it? Are there some structural faults? Could it be the bricks? So when I am writing a paper I will quote a theory. Theorems in mathematics are formulated very precisely so that I can refer to it and skip some steps of the proof. It is desirable that I know what other persons are doing but time is finite. Ideally one should be able to do it (i.e. check the proof) but it is not possible all the time. By working through examples we develop a kind of intuition of what should be true and what should be false. What is expected of us is to make as clear as possible which chains you are adding to the argument to make it as clear as possible for the others so that others can follow what has been done.

In the narrative the informant uses the metaphor of building a house to illustrate the role of trust in mathematics. Mathematicians build on the theorems of others and need to trust in this work partly because of the difficulty of developing a proof. Some mathematical theorems are relatively simple to prove, such as Pythagoras' theorem. Others literally take centuries to prove. One of the most famous and celebrated cases has involved the development of a proof for Fermat's last theorem. Pierre de Fermat was a seventeenth-century French mathematician who claimed that the margins of his notebook were too narrow to write down the proof for his last theorem. The complexity of this theorem took mathematicians over 350 years to prove. Eventually, a British mathematician, Andrew Wiles, took seven years to develop a 200-page proof of Fermat's last theorem (Kolata, 1993). The key point is that, in the interim, mathematicians had been reliant on the work of Fermat despite having no incontrovertible proof that it was correct. They had to trust the theorem before they could prove it beyond doubt. While there can never be any guarantee that someone has got the knowledge claim "right," sincerity is a precondition for meaningful progress and dialogue across all disciplines.

CONCEALMENT AND EXAGGERATION

The expectation of originality clearly creates a pressure that can tempt researchers into *concealment* or *exaggeration*. While there have been other high-profile cases of academic fraud it is important not to lose sight of more subtle and, perhaps, more common temptations associated with these vices. *Concealment* and *exaggeration* are twin vices that can occur where a researcher cannot resist emphasizing some results or masking others, perhaps confirming his or her theoretical or ideological stance, at the expense of other observations that may contradict cherished opinions or hypotheses.

Concealment can take many forms. One of these is sometimes referred to as "(data) trimming." Researchers will often generate large quantities of "data" through experiments, responses to questionnaires, interviews, and observations. Determining how to analyze and present "findings" almost invariably involves a process of discrimination and selection. A routine but difficult decision is how to "trim" the data. This means that a selection needs to be made on a rational basis, sometimes justified through statistical sampling techniques. Choosing what to omit is rarely an easy decision. While research may give the appearance or air of being true it should also be underpinned by evidence of its verisimilitude (Hillier & Jameson, 2003). However, trimming can occur in order to ensure that it excludes data which contradicts a thesis, argument, or hypothesis. This phenomenon is often illustrated by the case of Nobel Prize-winning physicist Robert Millikan who chose to omit some of his oil drop experiments in his reporting. While it is agreed that Millikan developed valid results in his measurement of electron charges, his motives for omitting data are difficult to establish. It is probable, though, that he did so in order to obtain a result which had greater statistical significance.

However, it is important to understand that the Millikan case is an extreme example of falsification through concealment and exaggeration. Outright data falsification is far less common among researchers than deliberate omissions or oversights. A survey of early- to mid-stage career health scientists found that that very few confessed to having falsified research data but more than 12% admitted to having deliberately ignored the use of falsified data by other researchers (Martinson et al., 2005). This is referred to as "normal" or "mundane" misbehavior and relates to more fine-grained decisions about what is right and wrong (De Vries et al., 2006).

> It is particularly important to notice that when scientists talk about behaviors that compromise the integrity of their work . . . rather they mention more mundane (and more common) transgressions, and *they link these problems to the ambiguities and everyday demands of scientific research.* (De Vries et al., 2006, 48)

Hence, a more typical scenario facing researchers, and not just in the natural sciences, is whether to confront or overlook what one may believe to be the falsification of research data that forms an important part of the conceptual or theoretical basis for one's own work. Here, there may be a question as to whether the falsification by an academic peer is deliberate, or possibly inadvertent. The researcher may have no personal relationship with the author of the research upon which they are drawing and little or no access to their original research data. If they have doubts about the accuracy of the data they may simply discount the paper as insufficiently convincing to rely upon in their own study and not discuss it. However, circumstances can arise where previous research must be relied upon in order to take an academic problem forward. Such a scenario is illustrated in narrative 7.2 where concern about possible bias in the trimming of data in statistical tests occurs in the context of accountancy research.

Narrative 7.2

Trimming the Data

Together with my research partner, I have been working on an empirical paper that investigates the way in which accruals are valued in share price. Accruals are the changes that accountants make to the cash transactions that take place in a period in order to calculate profit. A paper came out recently on the reliability of accruals. We have adapted our paper to include the concept of reliability proposed by these authors. We are using the same data set and so just checked that we could replicate their results before testing our own more developed model. In empirical accounting research the trimming of data sets is very important as most variables are ratios and so can become very, very large if the denominator becomes very small. In the extreme it becomes infinite when the denominator is 0. In accounting many numbers can be close to zero, such as profit for example, and so trimming of data sets is very important to identify true underlying relationships. Normally the largest and smallest 1% of a data set is trimmed—that is the observations are ignored—in order to eliminate any bias from extreme values.

In this other paper the authors only explicitly explain how they trimmed some of the data. Their paper is written in such a way that it is very easy—we did it and others that we have asked also assumed the same as we did—to think that all variables are trimmed the same way. We contacted the authors, who we know vaguely, just to check and they claim that they cannot remember how they trimmed all of the variables. We were immediately suspicious as trimming is so important. When we ran our tests without trimming all of the variables we can get similar results to theirs. The trouble is that they are claiming a new breakthrough with their results but if you trim the variables their result not only disappears but it reverses. We are suspicious that they knew this and therefore wrote the paper in the obfuscated way that they did to disguise the fact that their results are very suspect. We are now in a quandary because the new model we have developed suggests that their results are incorrect and we would have to explain the difference in results and basically accuse them of cheating.

Concealment is not just about the misrepresentation of "hard" data. It may be associated with researchers who harbor an undeclared political or ideological agenda, particularly, although not limited to, those working in the humanities and social sciences. Here, their research can be used as a tool to further a particular political perspective. Tooley (with Darby, 1998) suggests that educational researchers can be heavily

biased toward particular political positions without explicitly acknowledging the controversial nature of the position they are taking. Sometimes an unacknowledged value position can be revealed through an
idolization of particular authors who may not always be relevant to
the research at hand. Arguably, all research is premised on some form
of partisanship. To avoid the type of criticism made by Tooley it is
important that researchers openly acknowledge their underlying value
positions (Yorke, 1999).

Sometimes a researcher can be tempted to exaggerate the extent to
which a pattern may be emerging in results and can enter into a process
which is consciously and, perhaps, sub-consciously self-deceptive as
well as deceptive to others. Relatively subtle decisions regarding data
analysis or other forms of interpretation can "skew" or "bias" the
results of research toward a pattern that conforms with the beliefs
or expectations of the researcher. Here, it is important to understand
that concealment or exaggeration is often far from deliberate since our
assumptions about what is important to "look for" in a data set can
be shaped by our values or attitudes. Unfortunately, human fallibility
can mean overlooking more significant but unanticipated, or perhaps
unwanted, results. Homan draws on his own personal experience in a
candid admission of the way this vice can operate.

> The author of this book has known the experience of working
> through over 200 questionnaires and noticing halfway through
> that a pattern is emerging that would be at least newsworthy.
> From that moment, he opened envelopes hoping for responses
> that would lend themselves to such findings. The temptation is to
> resolve ambiguous replies in one's favor. And when the intention
> had been to group respondents within five equal ranges on a
> 100-point scale, there was a temptation to re-group these in four
> categories covering the same range when a large number of
> respondents fell between 76 and 80. He hopes that he did not
> yield and that the precaution against distorted interpretation was
> the retention of returned questionnaires for secondary analysis.
> (Homan, 1991, 8)

The frank illustration provided by Homan is perhaps closer to the
real, everyday temptations of the research creation process than the
more "extreme" examples of academic fraud that make good headlines.
Exaggeration is further connected with claims that researchers might
make that extend beyond the particular set of conditions or circumstances that pertain to their research study. Sometimes research studies
may show a particularly promising result on the basis of one, limited

research sample. For example, children in one particular school may show a marked improvement in their academic work through the application of a new teaching technique, or the condition of patients suffering from a medical condition may react favorably to a new drug. Such results raise questions about the extent to which it can be claimed that these results may be "generalizable." In other words, is it possible to exercise sufficient control over the relevant "factors," such as the personality of the teacher(s) or the composition of the student class by age, class, race, gender, and other differences, to make a universal claim? Similarly, is the patient group "typical" of the wider population?

Researchers often seek to claim that the results of their research are generalizable on the basis that the sample selected for the original study is reflective of the relative wider population. They tend to do this by using larger samples and adopting quantitative rather than qualitative methodologies and techniques of analysis. This enables them to make broader claims about the importance or significance of their research. Simply using larger samples, though, does not always mean that researchers are generating more "significant" results. Sometimes a technique can be deployed for inflating the probability by using a sample size that is unnecessarily large. This can result in a weak effect being statistically enhanced (Rugg & Petre, 2004). Sometimes researchers may claim that they have found out something that is "significant." The use of this word though is also open to abuse. In a specialized statistical sense the use of the word "significant" implies that the chance of something happening at random is, at most, just 1 in 20 (Rugg & Petre, 2004).

If researchers cannot make claims about the generalizability of their research this tends to put them at a disadvantage both in terms of the esteem in which their research is held and their ability to secure funding or satisfy sponsors. Their research may be considered unfavorably or dismissed as "too small scale," "just a case study," "only local" or "essentially parochial." Research sponsors want research which traverses the limitations of place and space including national contexts and disciplines. In a study of policy-makers connected with the United Nations and other international agencies, Williams and Robinson (2007, 9) state that "research is influential if it is generalizable."

Evidence further suggests that many research sponsors tend to favor quantitative methods of data collection as a means of demonstrating generalizability. This has been reflected by the deepening bias in social and educational research in favor of quantitative approaches. Policy-making bodies historically prefer to fund research based on such methods (Finch, 1986). Writing about public education systems,

Lingard and Blackmore (1997, 8) argue that quantitative research is favoured over qualitative because of its claims to be more "generalisable and predictive." An influential report into the state of educational research in the UK in the late 1990s (Tooley with Darby, 1998) questioned the quality and "usefulness" of educational research. Much of the criticism was centered on a reliance on qualitative, non-empirical work and has led to an increased emphasis on "evidence-based" research within the education field. Similar debates have occurred in other disciplines. Researchers who pin their colors to the mast of a particular qualitative method find themselves increasingly maginalized as the ability to generate research grant income has become an ever more central consideration in career progression opportunities. The "impact" of research on practice is one of the criteria being applied in respect of the 2008 UK Research Assessment Exercise (see chapter 10). Making claims about "impact" places researchers under pressure to give examples of where their work has been cited, used, or applied by others both at a national and international level. Such assertions tend to be easier to make if research is generalizable beyond its immediate context or location. The extent to which research traverses national boundaries is also an "esteem" indicator for an academic, demonstrating that their work is internationally influential. This context means that there are significant pressures on researchers to make claims regarding the extent to which their results are generalizable and of significance on both a national and international basis. These expectations can lead to exaggeration as a means of satisfying such demands.

The temptation to exaggerate some findings and conceal others is understandable in a context in which prestige, research funding, and career prospects attach to originality. A further example of how the virtue of sincerity may be eroded is the use of exaggeration as a mechanism to build a personal reputation on the basis of seeking to contradict or discredit a rival theory. The alleged shortcomings of previous research in time, space, scope, or theoretical assumptions will often underpin a research project. Here there can be a danger that the real objective of the research is to discredit the work of rival academics or academic theories rather than focusing on answering the research question.

SINCERITY AND AUTHENTICITY

Authenticity is a word sometimes employed as a synonym for sincerity and is attracting growing attention in philosophy and education (e.g. Taylor 1991; Barnett 2007; Kreber et al., 2007). One of the tensions at the heart of our conventional understanding of "good" research is the need for the researcher to be "impartial," "objective," and even "neutral" or "detached" (Brew, 2001a) whilst, at the same time, producing work that is an "authentic" representation of their own beliefs and values. However, to be authentic it is unreasonable to expect people to be "neutral" since authenticity demands being aware of our own "inner feelings" (Taylor, 1991). This is about what is sometimes referred to as meta-cognitive awareness; getting to know who we are and who we want to become.

In more narrow research terms, authenticity implies that the researcher has integrity and their data can be trusted. In broader terms, research that claims to be authentic is likely to be "dishevelled by its very complexity" (Senior & Hay, 2005). The temptation for any researcher, however, is to "dress up" their findings in some way in order to give it face validity to their target readership. For example, it is conventional for researchers to preface the results section of research papers with some kind of a review of the literature. This normally seeks to demonstrate, in part, why the need for the study has arisen, often on the basis of claims that previous research may be inadequate, insufficiently robust, or simply in need of up-dating or extension. The reader, in short, is given the impression that the research design flows from the analysis of the literature. This may not, though, be a safe assumption as it is not unusual for the literature review to be written up after, rather than before, the data has been collected, sometimes by another person, such as a research assistant rather than the principal investigator. While there may not be an explicit intention to deceive, such practices can give the reader the false impression that the empirical study was designed to interrogate broader theories or conceptions (Mills, 1970). Presenting findings in a truly authentic way demands courage to resist pressures to make research appear falsely "neat," "tidy," or simply linear.

Making results generalizable is just one of a number of pressures on researchers that encourages inauthentic or insincere behavior. Brew (2001a) identifies 15 "traditional rules" of research several of which can lead to a lack of authenticity in academic work. A simple, but nonetheless powerful example is provided by the expectation that research should be supported by "lots of references" (Brew, 2001a). Another "rule" related to this one is that as a researcher you "must sound like you have read the book." The acknowledgment of the influence and originality of others is a fundamental rule of intellectual integrity. Students inducted into higher education are invariably warned about the need to comply with this expectation from the very beginning of their academic careers. Referencing is seen as essential as a means of acknowledging the intellectual debt owed to others. However, the art of referencing can be deployed in a number of circumstances that are essentially inauthentic or not true to a sincere application of this convention. Researchers, for example, will frequently reference sources they have not read. There are a numbers of reasons for this practice, such as using a reference obtained from reading someone else's article or book. Sometimes a researcher may have worked collaboratively with others and so is reliant on someone else having read the source cited. Another explanation of failing (in part) to read what one cites may arise if a researcher has relied on an abstract or extract rather than reading the source in its entirety. More fundamentally, referencing is all too often used to legitimize without any other form of proof. Such a practice lends a verisimilitude to a piece of research without automatically making it any more authentic. While these forms of behavior are not necessarily viewed as "unethical" they can give rise, deliberately or unintentionally, to a false impression as to the extent to which the researcher has genuinely engaged with the literature which he or she is seeking to build on or interact with. They are, as such, inauthentic forms of behavior.

There are other ways in which data is presented that serve as examples of inauthentic behavior especially in relation to "writing up." Another of Brew's (2001a) tongue-in-cheek "rules" is that research must represent "an academic discourse." This refers to the way in which research conforms to certain linguistic and stylistic conventions used within a discipline when it is presented. A distinction here may be drawn between "narration," as the literal telling of a story, and "narrative," which is what is actually recounted by the writer (Eagleton, 1996). Qualitative researchers may thus eliminate elements of a story that do not serve their subsequent purposes in reporting. This leads to accusations that they mask the inadequacies of their fieldwork by a skilful, yet inauthentic, writing style (Senior & Hay, 2005). Similarly, researchers who rely on quantitative techniques may be charged with using charts, tables, and figures to similar ends.

Examples have been given in this section of the way concealment and exaggeration operate on a sliding scale from virtue to vice rather than as fixed points of "right" or "wrong." Some of the behaviors described are accepted academic conventions and few researchers would claim never to have deployed some of these techniques to bolster the impression of authenticity. This does not necessarily make them dishonest but indicates that academic forms of communication do not always encourage authentic behavior in the reporting of research.

CONCLUSION

Sincerity is central to the pursuit of truth in research. Every researcher must live out this virtue since much of what may appear to be authentic can, in fact, be inauthentic behavior. Often it will only be the researcher who will ever know the truth behind the fine-grained decisions that are taken and this is an example of where excellence of character is the only real determinant of research ethics. The researcher must also live with the uncertainty associated with the pursuit of truth and the process of criticism that will permanently interrogate the claims to truth they might make. This critical process weakens the sense that truth is secure or unqualified but nonetheless, it is the engine that ultimately assures human progress.

8

HUMILITY

In science, each of us knows that what he has accomplished will be antiquated in ten, twenty, fifty years ... Every scientific "fulfillment" raises new "questions"; it asks to be "surpassed" and outdated. Whoever wishes to serve science has to resign himself to this fact. (Weber, 1973b, 61)

INTRODUCTION

The standard requirement for the attainment of a doctoral qualification is to make an original contribution in a knowledge field (Noble, 1994). In truth, few academics produce research which genuinely breaks completely new ground in the sense of creating an original theorem, process, or discovery. Academic research is undertaken in highly specialized fields. The results of these endeavors are often modest. They are more likely to provide fresh insights, critiques, and future directions rather than new theorems or discoveries. This does not mean that such work is trivial but that it is important not to overstate its significance. Even where research produces something insightful it may quickly become outdated or overtaken by new research.

The short shelf-life of academic research is not a new phenomenon. Writing in 1919, Max Weber recognized that the increasingly specialized nature of research meant that achievements in research were correspondingly incremental in nature. It is the fate of most researchers that the "glory" of their contribution to a research field will be invariably short-lived if ever substantially recognized by peers. The process of academic criticism is a continuous one and means that most researchers will only ever make minor and largely fleeting contributions to the stock of human knowledge. This stark reality means that researchers need to exercise the virtue of humility in the context of the dissemination phase of the research process.

THE IMPORTANCE OF DISSEMINATION

For research to be made meaningful it must be opened up to some form of scrutiny within the academic community or, perhaps, more widely to the general public. Depending on one's discipline or professional field dissemination might involve some form of publication, performance, or display. Examples include articles in learned journals, books, conference papers, musical recitals, or exhibitions of artistic artefacts. The range of possibilities for dissemination have been increased by the arrival of the World Wide Web and the possibilities this technology has opened up for the development of websites, web-blogs, emails, and electronic access to reports, articles, books, and other on-line resources. It is also now quite routine for academic authors to be asked by some publishers whether they would like to give open access to their papers on publication. But while we may be able to disseminate more than ever, is anyone interested? The exponential increase in research productivity worldwide in the last 30 years means that competition for the attention of our peers has never been greater. The challenge for the contemporary researcher is to find the most effective way to reach his or her intended readership or audience. There is a clear practical case for dissemination: to make one's research findings known, to gain feedback on these ideas from peers, and to gain recognition for one's work. Why, though, should one feel obliged to share research findings with others? There are a number of reasons why dissemination is important on moral grounds.

The first ground is what Merton (1973c) referred to as the institutional "norm" of communism. Stripped of its associations with political systems, Merton uses the word to refer to the common ownership of (scientific) goods. The sharing of knowledge and learning produced through academic endeavor is part of the collaborative spirit of the scientific or academic community. While Merton referred to "science" and "scientists" he did not use this term in a narrow sense and his norms, including communism, are applicable to all academics. According to Merton, the only sense in which a scientist can lay claim to "his" own intellectual property is with regard to the recognition and esteem which is attached to having created it (1973c, 273). The notion of communism in academic life, one of a number of "norms" identified by Merton, stands in stark contrast with the contemporary emphasis on the protection of intellectual property rights in respect to academic research.

> The communism of the scientific ethos is incompatible with the definition of technology as 'private property' in a capitalistic economy. (Merton, 1973c, 275)

Sharing academic knowledge makes it possible for knowledge to be critiqued by others and then, possibly, applied for the public good. Another, more modern way of looking at dissemination is that this is an obligation owed to a variety of "stakeholders" in the interests of human research subjects, colleagues within the discipline or profession, funding bodies and employers, and society at large (Hazlehurst, 2004). At a more prosaic level, researchers may be expected to disseminate their work under the terms of contracts or grant agreements with employers, funding bodies, or other private and public sponsors. Normally, sponsors wish to see researchers maximize the "impact" of their research through widespread dissemination across a variety of media.

However, the reverse of this situation may also apply especially for those engaged in research with commercial applications. Here, sponsors may choose to suppress research findings especially when they are deemed to be contrary to their interests. The single largest sponsor of medical research in the USA, UK, and Canada, the pharmaceutical industry, has been widely accused of such behavior (Baird, 2003). Moreover, a common condition of industrial sponsorship is that the results of research need to be kept secret for long enough for a company to determine whether or not to apply for a patent (Bok, 2003). This means that academic researchers in the biosciences can, in effect, be prevented from disseminating their research findings. Universities are also increasingly alive to the commercial value of research and are keen to encourage academics to realize such commercial potential through the protection of intellectual property rights. Some elements of this practice, including the application for patents and exclusive licences, are arguably contrary to the academic norm of communism as outlined by Merton. At the extreme, some critics of the modern university perceive a danger that academic departments are being transformed into little more than the research and development agencies of commercial organizations (Lucas, 1996).

DEGREES OF KNOWING

In disseminating research the central virtue is *humility*. This is about being self-effacing in relation to one's own contribution to the

advancement of knowledge. Research, however large-scale or longitudinal, rarely results in answering all the questions or problems which
have been identified. In this sense, research is always incomplete: an
ongoing process which can span generations of researchers, rather than a
one-off event. In reporting or disseminating research it is important,
therefore, to acknowledge what has been discovered and what still
remains undiscovered; to identify what a researcher feels has been
achieved and what remains to be done. There are degrees of knowing,
rather than, necessarily, absolute certainty. This reality requires the exercise of the virtue of humility and striking a balance between the extremes
of timidity, in being not prepared to report any findings, and boastfulness, in over-stating one's achievements in breaking new ground.

Humility demands, among other things, a respect for the work of
others that have gone before and a recognition of the limitations, of
one's own contribution and potentially of the limitations of one's previous accuracy. That is why it is customary in academic research to
present one's own findings in the context of the work of others. This
virtue is inculcated into students from the very start of their university
studies. A failure to cite others is at best poor scholarship or at worst
plagiarism if we claim the ideas of others as our own. This is about
intellectual integrity. It is not just polite to cite other authors but essential in establishing the extent to which one may have added to the
current stock of knowledge or taken issue with established perspectives.

Humility is recognized by Merton (1973d) as another one of his
"institutional norms" associated with both the social and human sciences. Merton explains this virtue (or "norm," in his terms) as about
paying "homage to those who have prepared the way for one's own
work" (p303). Schwehn (1993) identifies humility in a similar way to
Merton as a virtue that demonstrates a respect for the work of others.
He argues that contemporary students are sometimes too quick to
dismiss other authors as difficult to understand when a more humble
attitude would be to consider whether the apparent inaccessibility of
an author might, in fact, be due to the reader's inadequacies. If one
respects and takes seriously the work of others it follows that one is
prepared to evaluate the accuracy of one's own beliefs or research
results. Here, Schwehn identifies humility as a preparedness to "abandon some of our most cherished beliefs" (p49). In this context, humility
is associated with being capable of changing one's mind. For example,
a piece of research may demonstrate the inadequacy or inaccuracy of
one's own previous work on a subject.

A researcher needs to consider the extent to which their findings or
results may be relied upon to provide complete or partial answers to

research problems and questions. Here, the researcher recognizes that research is an ongoing process and that findings may be provisional rather than incontrovertible. This type of circumspection is important in order to avoid accusations of exaggeration (see chapter 7). Often, when presenting a paper researchers will deploy a circumspect language that uses phrases such as "work in progress," "provisional findings," or "tentative conclusions." This is not just coyness. It is about being humble and explicit about the extent to which they are confident in making new claims to knowledge. In many disciplines it is customary to use this lexicon of circumspection at the conclusion of a research paper and particularly when presenting conference papers.

Most academic papers will conventionally contain commentaries, often found in methodology or results sections, critiquing their own shortcomings. This may be illustrated by reference to a paper about gender differences in attitudes to business ethics. Statistical analysis from this study identifies that women "are less likely than men to act in the same (unethical) way presented in the scenarios as indicated by the significant difference between men and women in the mean for intention to behave" (Stedman et al., 2007, 171). In short, the study suggests that women are more "ethical" than men when faced with particular business scenarios. However, the authors of the paper are also concerned to summarize the limitations of their own study in the following terms:

> In interpreting the results of this study, certain limitations need to be considered. First the sample is rather small . . . Second, the results are not easily generalized. The sample is drawn from one country only. Furthermore, the sample, graduate business students, may not be representative of the population overall. Third, the ethics measure was developed in the United States and may be somewhat culture-bound. Fourth, the questionnaire was in English which was not the respondents' first language. These limitations notwithstanding, the results of this study contribute to the ethics literature by enhancing our understanding of gender differences in ethical analysis. (Stedman et al., 2007, 172)

The limitations which are identified by Stedman and her colleagues are typical of those of many research investigations, such as the size of the sample and the extent to which it is representative of the relevant population as a whole. In this particular example, the researchers drew on a sample of German business students and further acknowledged the implications of relying on a single national group and the possible linguistic issues of asking this sample to complete a questionnaire in English, rather than in their native German.

Crucially, such limitations have implications for the extent to which claims may be generalized beyond the immediate context in which they were generated. Being able to "universalize" the findings from research in this way is critical to academic reputation (see chapter 7). According to Merton, the norm of universalism requires the application of "preestablished impersonal criteria" (Merton, 1973c, 270) in judging the validity of knowledge claims. This norm asserts the importance of staying detached and analyzing all data in an objective way enabling the creation of universal or objective knowledge. In this way, truth claims may be said to transcend race, class, political, and/or religious barriers. Universalism is not just a key academic norm for those committed to the quantitative philosophy of "big science." It is also a value shared by many contemporary academics working in a broad range of disciplines, including the social sciences and humanities (Macfarlane & Cheng, 2008).

> The Haber process [the scientific method of producing ammonia developed during World War II] cannot be invalidated by a Nuremberg decree nor can an Anglophobe repeal the law of gravitation. (Merton, 1973c, 270)

INTELLECTUAL DEBTS

Acknowledging the contribution of others in developing our research is also a facet of humility. The paper by Stedman and her colleagues helps to illustrate the way that researchers acknowledge their intellectual debt to others both in their immediate field, in this case, business ethics research, and those in adjoining or contributing cognate areas. The paper lists 48 references, only just over half of which refer to articles in business ethics journals. The others represent the work of scholars and researchers in moral and social philosophy, organizational and behavioral theory, and psychology, including influential figures in gender studies and the theory of moral development (Carol Gilligan and Lawrence Kohlberg, respectively).

It is commonplace to find an "acknowledgments" section at the start of a book (such as this one) and a list of research articles. This, again, is more than about common courtesy. It represents an attempt to acknowledge the intellectual contribution of others who may not necessarily be listed as co-authors. Such individuals frequently include postgraduate degree supervisors, anonymous reviewers and peers who have commented on drafts of the manuscript, research assistants, and research subjects acknowledging both their co-operation and intellectual insights. Research papers in the "hard" sciences are frequently multi-authored, reflecting the teamwork that goes into collecting and analyzing large data sets. In Lisa Lucas' book *The Research Game in Academic Life* one of her interviewees comments on the way he felt it only right to include the names of his co-researchers despite the fact that single-authored papers carry a higher premium for individuals looking to gain prestige and kudos.

> Dr Stanton produced a lot of papers that were mainly multi-authored. He was criticized for this in the department. However, his research, firstly, was dependent on one particular professor (at another university) for the materials he needs for research. So this person must always be cited in his work. Secondly, he felt he should help people in their careers. So he included the names of his research staff. (Lucas, 2006, 141)

In the context of the UK Research Assessment Exercise, the fastidious-ness of Dr Stanton in ensuring that all contributors were duly recognized through a co-authorship credit meant that he effectively diminished his own scholarly "profile." Such profiles result from being the only named, or sometimes either first or last named author on an academic paper. Emphasizing collaboration and being modest about one's own contribution are sadly contrary to the way blunt-edged assessments of academic work place particular stress on the achievements of an indi-vidual researcher. This is creating an incentive for modern researchers to be boastful, rather than humble.

BOASTFULNESS

Like all the virtues it is possible to be insufficiently humble or go too far in claim-making on behalf of one's research. At this end of the spectrum is the vice of *boastfulness* which occurs when a researcher has a deficiency of humility. This may result in someone over-stating the extent to which their work is significant in terms of creativity, originality, utility, or applicability across contexts. It can also manifest itself in a number of other ways. Self-regarding behavior such as exces-sive self-citation of the researcher's previous work and co-citation through mutual agreement with others are further examples of boastful behavior that illustrate this vice (see chapter 10). All researchers tend to self-cite to some extent as a legitimate means of building on previous work. It is important to draw the line, though, where this practice becomes self-serving or egocentric in nature. In different analyses of citation practice across disciplines it has been noted that self-citation can often inflate the relative importance of a particular author (e.g. Hyland, 2001; Tight, 2005).

In reviewing the papers of others, academics are placed in a powerful position to make judgments about the merit of the work of fellow researchers that may have a direct effect on their academic careers. Some reviewers tend to be "assassins" (Siegelman, 1991), mainly recommending rejection and applying tough and exacting standards. Others, at the opposite end of the spectrum, may adopt a more lenient attitude. These "zealots" (Siegelman, 1991) are much more likely to accept than reject a manuscript. The review process is inevitably subjective as personalities and benchmarks of appropriate standards will differ between individuals. However, in the exercise of judgment reviewers face a number of particular temptations. One of these is the desire of some reviewers to see more papers published from their own particular area of expertise. Siegelman's (1991) study of reviewer behavior indicates that this is a motivation behind the leniency of some zealots. An opposite emotion is expressed by the temptation to reject papers that do not conform with one's own value position or belief system or, even worse, simply because of a personal dislike for another academic. The latter type of behavior, one might think, ought not to be possible as most academic journals anonymize manuscripts sent to reviewers. Simply removing the name(s) of the author(s) though is no guarantee that their identity will not be detected through style, argument or, often, self-citation. Other more Machiavellian motives may be present in rejecting a paper. These include blocking the path of another researcher to ensure that one's own work about the same topic or problem gets into print first. Such malevolent tactics are designed to ensure that the reviewer rather than the rejected author is credited with "priority" in making a discovery or new intellectual contribution.

The vice of boastfulness may operate in peer-reviewing processes when recommendations for corrections and improvements to a manuscript include excessive or unjustified citation of the reviewer's own publications. Another way that this vice might operate is illustrated in the following narrative (narrative 8.1).

Narrative 8.1

A Tempting Citation

I was asked to review a journal article submitted to a leading journal in my field. I suspected that the editor asked me to undertake the review as the article made significant use of my research based on a presentation I made at a recent conference he had attended.

> I did not think that the article was very good because there were some leaps of logic and the main argument was neither convincing nor persuasive.
>
> My dilemma was whether to recommend the article for publication. It would have been very helpful to me to have an article by another author which showcased my research published in this prestigious journal. The citation in a prestigious journal would have been flattering and help to raise my research profile. However, the article was poor and it would have been disingenuous of me to have recommended it for publication. I decided to recommend that the article should not be published.

This narrative demonstrates that there can be a temptation to recommend a paper for publication on the basis that it already includes flattering references to one's own research. While, in this instance, my informant indicated that the paper was insufficiently strong in other respects to be recommended, the temptation still exists.

> Peer reviewing and refereeing are . . . often ineffectual, and in some respects corrupt, infested with politics, rife with temptation to plagiarise. (Judson, 2004, 7)

Part of the problem, as Judson recognizes, lies in the recent, rapid growth in the number of journals and greater competition between academics. This has made it necessary for editors to expand their pool of reviewers or allow a practice known as "pyramiding." Here, established members of the review board ask other academics they know to review papers, making the process both more cliquish and less transparent. Competitive pressures in academic life to publish or publish more are associated with a questioning of the originality of some contributions.

Authorship disputes can take many forms. Some of the most dramatic cases involve disputes over whether an author has taken false credit for someone else's intellectual work or discovery. However, more commonplace quarrels tend to surround the order in which the names of authors appear when a publication appears. To the uninitiated, such a concern may seem rather trivial and petty but the order that names appear in on a publication raises issues beyond personal vanity. For example, in some national contexts doctoral students in a number of disciplines must have a refereed publication as a first author before they can be awarded a PhD.

Being the first named author is about academic prestige and is an example of the "symbolic capital of renown" (Bourdieu, 1988, 79). Bourdieu identified a number of other forms of "capital" that directly relate to status and authority in academic life. These include the economic capital that derives from having access to sources of income and assets, such as obtaining research grants; the social capital of belonging to durable and influential academic groups, networks, and cliques; and the cultural capital that comes from possessing a range of knowledge and skills, such as the high social status that can stem from having attended a prestigious education institution. In practical terms, being the first named author in a co-authored paper is an important indicator of esteem.

Narrative 8.2

Getting the Order Right

Most of the research that I have undertaken into aspects of learning, teaching, and assessment in higher education has been on a collaborative basis. Consequently, it has been necessary to agree the order in which my name and those of my colleagues will appear, when the results of our research are put into the public domain by means of conference papers or journal articles. In general, this has been settled amicably with the person contributing most or, in the case of action research projects, owning the particular issue or problem, being the first named author.

On one occasion, however, a dispute arose over this. I thought that my name should come first. This was because I had done most of the research in terms of the trawling of the literature and raising and resolving some of the key questions. In addition, I had drafted much of the article, with my two co-authors simply offering comments and suggestions for me to consider in writing the final version. My assumption about the ordering of names, however, was challenged by one of my co-authors. He felt that, since the project was originally his idea, he should head the list of authors, even though he had effectively handed over responsibility to me. Eventually, so as not to hold up the submission of the article to a journal, he relented but with a certain amount of bad grace. This inevitably led to future difficulties in our professional relationship and, once some ongoing projects had been completed, no further collaboration.

As a result of this experience I have always sought to raise the issue of the order in which names will appear at a relatively early stage. I have also used it as an opportunity for discussing, particularly with those who are new to research, the obligations and tasks attached to their likely position in the list of authors. This avoids the danger of seeing the order of names as something which is entirely separate from other aspects of the project.

In narrative 8.2 the informant felt that his name should have gone first as he had "done most of the research in terms of the trawling of the literature and raising and resolving some of the key questions." While in this particular situation, the informant, an academic, was able to impose his will on the situation and ensure that his contribution was recognized through becoming the first named author, this will not necessarily always be the outcome. Here, an all too familiar scenario is that a student research assistant, who may have done the majority of the data-gathering or analysis, is given insufficient authorship credit or, at worst, does not even receive an acknowledgment in the published paper. Good doctoral supervisors will recognize and not seek to exploit the power imbalance between them and their graduate students. Others though are less scrupulous and can take excessive credit where it is not due to them.

Private sector organizations will sometimes look to utilize the reputation of established academics to give "credibility" to research findings that cast a favorable light on their own organization or practices they wish to promote. In the narrative "Credit where credit is due" (see narrative 8.3), a freelance economist did statistical work which was then incorporated into an academic paper published under the sole name of a well-known academic economist. While the freelance economist was paid a fee for his efforts, he was still left feeling cheated by the absence of any acknowledgment. Here, it is important to understand that plagiarism is a common phenomenon in corporate life as well as academia (Nitterhouse, 2003). Plagiarism in professional and business organizations occurs where someone in a more senior position takes credit for the work of someone in a more junior position who is the true author of a business idea, strategy document, or research report.

Narrative 8.3

Credit where Credit is Due

I was working as a freelance economist and was asked by an economic consultancy to carry out a statistical exercise to prove that the economic forecasts they provided were superior to others. This required me to do a vast amount of data collection, which I needed to input into various spreadsheets. Then I carried out a number of statistical calculations and provided a short paper. I was paid some £2,000 for this. The economic consultancy decided they needed a well-known academic expert in this specific field—a professor at a London university—to give the conclusions credibility. He wrote a paper, using my data collection and analysis using extra statistical tools, which was published in a reputable academic journal. It appeared under his name as sole author. This article was also sent by the consultancy to all its clients.

When I saw the published article I was surprised and a little annoyed. However, I was a little naïve in these things, but nevertheless contacted the economic consultancy to express my surprise. They communicated this to the Professor who apologized and said that next time they would acknowledge me. The professor who was a statistician rather than an economist was indeed the sole author. In a repeat exercise two years later there was an acknowledgment, though only for data collection.

The narrative may also be seen as an example of the so-called "Matthew Effect" (Merton, 1973d) in which eminent or famous academics will tend to receive more credit than comparatively unknown researchers. In other words, there is a cumulative effect of reputation and credit tends to be given disproportionately to those who are already well known. Some established researchers seek to mitigate the effects of this phenomenon by ensuring that academic credit is fairly distributed between collaborators. However, all too often, the most established "name" appears as the first author of a paper regardless of the extent to which they have contributed to a particular piece of research. This means that in subsequent citation, the other, perhaps more major contributors to multi-authored papers or books, are condemned to anonymity by the "et al." effect where only the first named author is identified in the text for ease of reference.

The Matthew Effect can operate in other ways. The imagery of the heroic scientist or inventor means that one person can be given undue credit for making a discovery whilst others who have made a significant contribution are overlooked. The attribution of credit to Alexander Fleming for the discovery of penicillin, for example, tends to over simplify and marginalize the role of others in making this scientific breakthrough. Sometimes a situation can arise where two researchers work on the same problem or question and come up with similar answers or solutions at the same time, either known or unknown to each other. Here, it is likely that credit will principally attach to the person with the more established academic reputation. The effect may also be seen in student work where they misattribute credit for original ideas to the authors of synoptic textbooks rather than the original sources upon which the textbooks draw.

TIMIDITY

At the other end of the spectrum, it is possible, though, to be too humble or circumspect in relation to the dissemination of one's research and this can manifest itself in the vice of *timidity*. Here, there is a failure to expose work to the interrogation of peers through a lack of confidence or a fear, perhaps, of criticism. Presenting conference papers, writing an article for a learned journal or displaying an artefact in a public space is about demanding, and sometimes receiving, critical attention. It can be an intimidating experience even for a seasoned researcher. However, being unwilling to enter into this process can damage the credibility of the claims made in one's research. It can also reflect poorly on the reputation of the researcher by failing to give the academic community the opportunity to comment, criticize, and, potentially, learn from the work in question. Beyond these considerations, there may be adverse implications in not reporting findings, however incomplete, as others will be unable to use this work to take their own research a stage further. Many important scientific breakthroughs result from the gradual accumulation of research findings, producing a solution for a particular problem by drawing on the incomplete findings of others. Here, there is a moral imperative to disseminate rather than to block the path to the truth. To do otherwise would be to reject through one's actions Merton's norm of communism.

Another aspect of timidity is the way academics can over-emphasize the language of circumspection, resulting in a veil of "ifs," "buts," "maybes," and quotations seeking to deflect attention from their own "voice." This inauthentic behavior (see chapter 7) is described by Barnett (2007, 45) as a tendency for both students and academics to "hide behind the 'they,' for there lies a sense of security. The bibliographies grow ever longer; the quotations proliferate and the commentaries on what B said about A proliferate." Such practices are not uncommon and, to some extent, are encouraged through formal academic training that frequently places a strong emphasis on the importance of referencing to sources and cautiousness in claim-making. Giving due credit to others as the originators of particular ideas is undoubtedly important. There is a risk, though, that the language of circumspection associated with excessive referencing practices can become more of a security-blanket designed to deflect potential criticism from one's own ideas.

CONCLUSION

Dissemination of research is essential to the development of human knowledge. A failure to disseminate can have serious consequences particularly in areas of academic study that relate to human health. Academics have an obligation to ensure that their work is opened up to scrutiny and a collegial duty to contribute to the growth of knowledge in their discipline. This demands self-discipline to publish at the right time rather than too early in pursuit of personal glory or too late to deliberately inhibit the progress of academic rivals. At the end of the dissemination phase, or perhaps even before, many academics will rush into fresh research projects driven by performative pressures (see chapter 10) or an energetic personality. Before starting a new project, however, a period of reflection can prove intellectually rewarding and can help to ensure that we are analyzing ourselves as rigorosly as we are analyzing our data. "Reflexivity" is a virtue that helps complete the research cycle and is the subject of the final chapter in this section of the book.

9

REFLEXIVITY

To be able to trust yet to be sceptical of your own experience, I have come to believe, is one mark of the mature workman. ... developing self-reflective habits you learn to keep your inner world awake. (Mills, 1970, 217)

INTRODUCTION

During the course of writing this book I have made a number of presentations at various seminars and conferences. This has provided me with valuable feedback on whether the virtues identified in the book resonate with other academics. It has enabled me to "reflect," as a result of which I have made a number of modifications during the course of writing. This has resulted in the addition of new chapters, the refinement of others and the further development of the virtues and vices. One of the comments I have received is that the virtue of "reflexivity" might be better placed at the beginning of the research cycle. It should, in other words, precede all the others. Clearly for those with previous experience of the research process this ought, ideally, to be the case since they would have matters on which to reflect. For new or inexperienced researchers, it may occur more naturally at a later point although, ideally, a researcher should be reflecting on their work on a continuous basis.

In this final chapter on the virtues of research, I will outline what reflexivity means and how it can be lived out both as an intellectual and moral virtue. The experience of having done a piece of research will lead us naturally to reflect on how well (or badly) it went. What worked? What did not work particularly well? How could I do it better next time? These are the kind of questions that most researchers ask themselves at regular intervals. The ways we can approach thinking about these kind of questions will ultimately determine how good we are as researchers.

MAKING THE TACIT EXPLICIT

Sometimes there is a tendency to present "research" as a depersonalized process where the researcher is expected to behave in a detached, rational, logical, and empirical manner. The emotional detachment of the researcher is another example of what Brew (2001a) terms as one of the "traditional rules" of the research process. This is, essentially, a "positivist" view of the nature of knowledge (see chapter 5). Yet, the intellectual and emotional demands of "doing" research call for a conscious and critical engagement with one's own performance. All (good) researchers will apply the academic norm of "organized skepticism" (Merton, 1973c) in relation to their own work. They will question, re-question, and seek to improve their method, style, analytical technique, presentation of results, and, indeed, anything that relates to how the research was conducted. As academics, researchers need to turn their critical instincts on themselves to the same degree that they interrogate the work of others.

> What I mean by self-reflective aware consciousness is that she would have used her feelings as a resource in her research and not suppressed them. (Brew, 2001a, 104)

A number of other authors have written about the meaning of reflexivity. Giddens (1984) defines this as an awareness about being more than simply self-conscious. He argues that as human beings we need to be able to elaborate on the reasons underpinning our activities. Hence, reflexivity is about articulating reasons for actions rather than just being aware of these motivations. Building on Giddens (1984), Hillier and Jameson (2003) define reflexivity as "the ability proactively to reflect, analyse and self-critically vocalise our own reflections while maintaining a critical awareness of the nature of culture and society around us" (p26). In other words, we must be able to give voice to our reflections, not merely keep them to ourselves.

However, being reflexive is about more than being honest or open. It involves analyzing and articulating thoughts and practices which we may well take for granted or are not particularly aware of. We may sub-consciously understand how we go about certain research activities, such as determining what hypothesis to choose, what questions to ask an interviewee, or how to analyze data, yet find this difficult to explain to ourselves or to others. The way that we have developed our research practices are based on experience "in the field." They are personal and context-specific practices. This type of understanding is sometimes called "tacit" knowledge as opposed to explicit knowledge which is written down or codified in some formal way (Eraut, 1994; Polanyi, 1967). A course or textbook on research methodology constitutes explicit knowledge, whereas much of how we research in practice relies on tacit knowledge. It exists but is not made explicit. Reflexivity is a skill, and also a virtue, that can make our tacit knowledge explicit.

Carla Willig (2001) distinguishes two types of reflexivity in relation to research: personal and epistemological. Personal reflexivity is about considering how the research process may have changed us as people by reshaping our thinking and beliefs as researchers. Other authors sometimes refer to the process of understanding the ways in which we learn as meta-cognitive awareness (Hillier & Jameson, 2003). Epistemological reflexivity requires us to interrogate critically the way in which we have conducted research through such things as the design of the study, the questions asked, and the analysis of the results. Reflexivity is about questioning ourselves and the way we have done things. What have we learnt from the research process? How have we developed as researchers? What things will we do differently next time? These are vital questions that all researchers need to keep asking themselves. Epistemological reflexivity supports the central process of truth-seeking since it is about thinking through how one might re-tackle a research problem or question.

Hence, the final phase of the research process involves thinking about what has gone right and what has gone wrong both in terms of epistemological issues and on a personal level. Here the virtue of *reflexivity* is about a self-awareness of the extent to which research undertaken has succeeded in terms of the researcher's own objectives.

While Willig (2001) contends that reflexivity is particularly important in qualitative research where there is greater recognition that a researcher cannot take an objectified "God's eye view" (Harraway, 1988), this virtue is important regardless of methodological predispositions. While reflexivity may be largely associated with the final stages of research, periods of reflection are valuable throughout the process. Janesick (1994) refers to the need for time for analysis and contemplation after a researcher has been immersed in the research setting for a period. This allows the researcher to consider the data collected carefully without, by implication, rushing into an immediate and possibly perfunctory judgment about the significance of the data or the story it tells.

Reflexivity might be considered an intellectual rather than moral virtue inasmuch that it involves a set of skills or procedures that can be learnt and improved through practice. However, such skills must be accompanied by a preparedness to open oneself up to criticism in the first place. This means that reflexivity is both an intellectual *and* a moral virtue.

DOGMATISM

The importance of reflexivity is reinforced in various ways by other writers concerned with the research process. Brew (2001a) identifies the importance of "looking again" as a rule for research, drawing on the work of Edward Husserl (1973). According to Husserl, "looking again and again is a way of minimizing self-deception" (1973, 58). Sometimes, however, researchers are not prepared to question their own performance in the conduct of research or consider critically how they might learn personal lessons. Such an attitude is about an epistemological and personal *dogmatism*, a vice that demonstrates a lack of reflexivity. For some researchers, their commitment to a particular ideological or theoretical position is so strong that they are not prepared to reconsider these opinions. Educational researchers, for example, are often criticized for pursuing research that "fits" their own ideological predispositions rather than pursuing work that might call their assumptions into question (Delamont, 2005). Methodology is also a key battleground where research training can inculcate commitment to a particular "camp." Here, there is a danger that commitment to a methodological faction can overwhelm the essential purpose of research in seeking an answer to a research problem or question (Murtonen & Lehtinen, 2005). This is a problem that is common to the framing (see chapter 4) and the reflexivity stages in the research cycle since they both involve an examination of one's own beliefs and values.

When methodology is accompanied by idolatory we end up with "methodolatory" (Janesick, 1994). This word is defined by Janesick (1994, 215) as "a preoccupation with selecting and defending methods to the exclusion of the actual substance of the story being told." It is about adulation for a particular method at the expense of all others and can often be linked to the political or ideological affiliations of the researcher and their world "view." The sociologist C. Wright Mills (1970) argued that dogmatic attachment to what he termed "The Scientific Method," derived from the natural sciences, masks weak and often trivial research which is over-reliant on statistical tests. In medical research, for example, large-scale randomized clinical trials have become a modern-day methodolatory. This is because such trials are widely viewed as the only legitimate means of determining the effectiveness and safety of a new drug. Mills contended that the dominance of what he termed abstracted empiricism meant that sociologists tended to lose sight of the broader social and economic context of their work. At the same time, Mills was critical of the dogmatism associated with "grand theory" which rejects empirical methods in favor of developing universal concepts that are often associated with unintelligible syntax and excessive devotion to particular theorists. Both abstracted empiricism and grand theory represent dogmatic positions. They are withdrawals into entrenched "camps" that inhibit, rather than promote, understanding of the contemporary world. It was for this reason that Mills was as opposed to the methodological inhibition of the empiricist as much as to the conceptual fetishism of the grand theorist. For both Mills and Janesick, the research question must always precede the desire to apply a particular methodology. The emphasis in research methodology training on developing an understanding of alternate philosophies of research design, often presented as "phenomenology" and "positivism" respectively, encourages researchers to become entrenched in a methodological "camp." Mills argued that researchers should be their own methodologists rather than becoming too attached to dogmatic positions.

Reflexivity requires researchers to be keenly self-aware of becoming rooted in dogmatic habits or attitudes. To reject the possibility of changing one's mind in academic life is to take an uncritical stance to the generation of knowledge and to put personal pride before the search for truth. Schwehn draws a parallel between the self-denial and self-sacrifice of the monk who gives up his soul in search of divine wisdom with that of the modern academic who gives himself up to the pursuit of the truth. A reflexive disposition requires us, at times, to be "prepared to abandon some of our most cherished beliefs" (Schwehn, 1993, 49). While Schwehn writes from a faith perspective, his analysis has much in common with Weber whose vision of academic life is based on a secular asceticism. For Weber, the academic must accept that whatever he might achieve in his lifetime will become quickly outmoded by the work of others (Shils, 1973). Appreciation of this reality means that the academic vocation is ultimately a self-sacrificing one. This means casting aside the personal vanity associated with academic priority and discovery in favor of supporting the continual search for truth and knowledge in common with others.

Dogmatism can also occur when researchers fail to follow the logical stages of the reflective process. Sometimes people can get "stuck" or jump a stage in the reflective process or cycle. According to Kolb (1984), this should involve a four-stage process: having an experience, reflecting on it, thinking about how relevant theory or other abstract ideas might help, and then implementing a new approach based on the conclusions you have reached. This cycle of reflection sounds ideal but, in reality, our personalities have a tendency of cutting the cycle short (Honey & Mumford, 1982). Those of us naturally inclined to personal reflection and observation may have a tendency to get stuck by failing to theorize or subsequently act on the basis of our reflections. Other individuals will happily theorize but find it more difficult or simply tend to exclude their own personal reflections. Then there are those who, eager to get on with things, will fail to take the time to either reflect or theorize before hastily putting a new plan into action. Clearly, personality comes into play in the way people reflect.

One of the steps recommended by Kolb that might be skipped due to impatience is that of abstract conceptualization or "theorizing." A new researcher may be unaware or only partially aware of their own operating assumptions. For example, they may be clear that they want to use a particular research instrument, such as a questionnaire, but might not have considered what factors underlie this decision in relation to their methodological disposition. In order for reflection to take place we need to have an awareness of our own personal stance (Brockbank & McGill, 1998). This is likely to develop and shift over time on the basis of experience.

INDECISIVENESS

At the other extreme to dogmatism lies *indecisiveness*, whereby reflexivity, if resulting purely in contemplation rather than any action, can stymie rather than facilitate future change and development in research practice. In the language of business, such a condition is sometimes referred to as "paralysis by analysis." Beyond a certain point, self-questioning and self-doubt become a destructive rather than a positive force, permanently damaging the confidence and purposefulness of the researcher. Becoming trapped in an indecisive frame of mind may, ultimately, lead to the researcher giving up. Epistemological reflexivity can also lead researchers down long and sometimes blind alleys that can lead to obfuscation rather than enlightenment. Research is often a process of trial and error but, arguably, it is only through repeated fieldwork that new experiences are acquired that help the researcher to reflect afresh. Getting the balance right between dogmatism and indecisiveness is ably summarized by C. Wright Mills in the following passage from *The Sociological Imagination*.

Thinking is a struggle for order and at the same time for comprehensiveness. You must not stop thinking too soon—or you will fail to know all that you should; you cannot leave it to go on for ever, or you yourself will burst. (Mills, 1970, 245)

OPPORTUNITIES FOR REFLECTION

Curiously, the concept of reflexivity is much more closely associated with teaching than with research. There have been countless books on the value of using reflection in relation to teaching and student learning (e.g. Brockbank & McGill, 1998). Even in books about research, reflection is seen primarily as a tool for thinking about teaching (Hillier & Jameson, 2003). It is a concept that is the cornerstone of many courses concerned with academic staff development. These invariably encourage participants to regard activities such as the keeping of a learning journal or being observed by a colleague as an opportunity to reflect and develop alternative teaching strategies. Many of the same opportunities exist for researchers (see figure 9.1) although we rarely tend to think of these parallel activities as having potential for reflection.

Opportunities for reflection can be both formal and informal and can take place on an individual as well as a group or collaborative basis. During the course of the research process individuals will have many opportunities for reflection, possibly resulting in changes in the way they conduct themselves, their methodology, or even the form of their analysis. This is normally referred to as reflection *in action*, as it occurs during the course of the activity itself. Things do not always go to plan and this

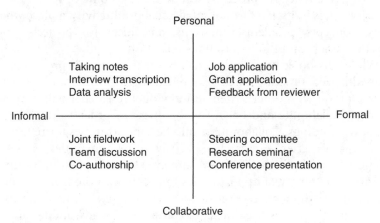

Figure 9.1 Examples of Opportunities for Reflection.
Based on Macfarlane & Ottewill, 2001.

demands flexibility on the part of the researcher. One example might be an interviewer who starts with a set of questions but realizes that, during the course of the interview, they need to adapt their approach and perhaps change their questions. Many experienced research interviewers prefer to use a small number rather than a large number of questions. This is because they have learnt that probing their interviewees further in a few areas is more effective than trying to cover too much ground. It can be the product of reflection in action but it may also be the product of reflection *on action*, where the interviewer has listened back to his or her own interview whilst transcribing an audio recording. In a similar way, during the course of data analysis a researcher might realize that one of their questions has been misinterpreted by respondents and that it needs to be rephrased or scrapped altogether. It is to allow for and address this type of problem that most experienced researchers will use a pilot interview or test out a questionnaire or experiment on a small scale before collecting data on a larger scale.

Other individualized activities, such as applying for a new academic position, can be inadvertent spurs to reflection about what someone has achieved, how successfully, and what they still need to accomplish in their academic career. More formally, a researcher might keep a journal or a "file" containing a range of sources for reflection. Such a file might contain "ideas, personal notes, excerpts from books, bibliographical items, and outlines of projects" as recommended by C. Wright Mills in writing about the concept of intellectual craftsmanship (1970, 219). While Mills' recommendations pertain to fellow sociologists they are equally relevant for academics from any discipline interested in engaging in a reflective process. Moreover, the keeping of such a file, as Mills saw it, is in itself a form of intellectual productivity, a place where facts, concepts, problems, questions, and ideas for projects come together as a prompt for continuous reflection.

While this book has focused mainly on the research process as an individualized process, much research involves formal and informal collaboration with others. Even an individual researcher will normally need to collaborate and engage with others in order to disseminate his or her findings. Collaboration enriches opportunities for reflection. Many may experience research, especially in the humanities and social sciences, as an individualized and sometimes lonely pursuit, but there are normally plenty of opportunities to reflect with the help of others. The acknowledgments section of theses, books, and academic papers are a guide to the positive impact of colleagues, friends, and families in what, in effect, is a reflective process (see chapter 6).

Supervising others may be regarded as a form of collaboration. This can formally result, on occasions, in joint authorship of academic papers between supervisor and research student. Informally, many supervisors speak of the way their relationship with a research student can shift from apprentice to peer during the course of time and the rich possibilities for co-learning. While there are ethical dimensions of such collaboration given inequalities in power relations, it is an important relationship for both parties. Furthermore, interaction with graduate students should be a spur for the supervisor to reflect on their own beliefs and practices, both as a teacher and in relation to the question or topic under scrutiny.

Presentations at research seminars and conferences, disseminating results or work in progress, can be productive in terms of evaluating one's progress and provide fresh insights from colleagues upon which to reflect. All too often presentations at such events are thought of as a one-way communication process rather than an opportunity for the researcher to gather critical reactions to their work. Researchers can be eager to tell people about their results using every available minute to "present." Approaching a presentation in an open manner in order to facilitate discussion demands greater courage but can potentially pro-duce much richer intellectual rewards than a didactic "delivery" of a series of visual aids designed to allow as little time for questions or dialogue as possible. A didactic style of presentation may symbolize nervousness or inexperience. It may also represent a dogmatic mind-set that is more intent on telling than on listening and gathering feedback for reflection.

A "steering" group or advisory committee will often be established to monitor the progress of a research project. For some funded projects it will frequently be a requirement. Peers with expertise in the cognate area will normally be members of such groups with a capacity to pro-vide expert advice and support to the research team. Here again, an unreflective or defensive mind-set may regard a steering group as an unwelcome imposition or source of interference while researchers with a more open attitude will regard such a grouping as an aid to reflection, with the help of others, on the progress they are making. Used appropriately, a steering group can act both as a support and a resource for discussing the challenges faced by a project team and help researchers to reflect in the process.

A NARRATIVE APPROACH

It is now increasingly possible to obtain a doctorate by publication rather than via a conventional thesis. This normally entails the submission of a series of linked peer-reviewed publications together with an overarching "narrative" that explains the contribution of the work to its field and the methodologies employed. In the arts field performances, artefacts, or compositions may be submitted for consideration rather than a journal paper or book. A PhD by publication is regarded by some as a more appropriate way to enable modern researchers to develop as academics as opposed to writing a lengthy thesis over several years that is unlikely to ever come to wider attention within the discipline or profession. Critics of this trend take the view that it represents a dilution of standards as there is no requirement to produce a single, extended thesis. However, others would contend that a PhD by publication represents work of equal intellectual value achieved by different means over time. The opportunity to gain recognition in this way better reflects the demands on contemporary academics and professionals to publish. Regardless of where one stands in this debate, the PhD by publication essentially represents the accreditation of prior learning on the basis of an adequate reflection on the nature of this learning.

The reflection takes place in the "narrative" or "overview" statement submitted to accompany and explain a candidate's publications which can normally vary in length between 5,000 and 20,000 words. This narrative demands that the researcher reflects systematically on her or his research presenting it as an integrated whole. They need to set out the context in which they have created their research, how it forms a coherent whole, at a conceptual, empirical, or perhaps methodological level, and identify how this work has contributed to the advancement of their discipline or professional field. The narrative requires considerable skill in reflection. Here, there is always a danger that this reflection can take on a self-justificatory tone in pressing the case that one's work represents original scholarship rather than being one that approaches the task of personal reappraisal in a more open manner. This requires that reflexivity is practiced both as an intellectual virtue, in communicating the coherence of one's research contribution, for example, and as a moral virtue by resisting the temptation to gloss over the trials, tribulations, and "false starts" that led to research results. Adopting a more honest and open approach to writing up such experiences will add a "richness" and a greater verisimilitude than a self-justificatory narrative. In other words, it will be a more accurate representation of the truth. It is also a way to return to the notion of tacit knowledge, of making this type of understanding in research explicit.

All the narratives contributed by academic colleagues to this book are, in themselves, an illustration of how an individual can formally reflect on their own research. Sometimes these include illustrations of the tacit knowledge that lies at the heart of being a researcher. This is not necessarily complex technical knowledge or particularly associated with methodology which is represented so strongly in our explicit or public knowledge about research. It often has much to do with the more human issues of politics and personalities (see narrative 9.1).

Narrative 9.1

Politics and Personalities

We had a multi-million dollar international research project with two co-chairs from different continents and many nationalities involved. The first major meeting was held in an ancient castle, and the opening plenary session was in a large baronial hall with a stage for the panel. One of the co-chairs opened the proceedings, and did not treat the other co-chair at all deferentially (the latter was from a culture where senior academics expect to be treated deferentially, not least in public).

After this opening session people went back to their rooms etc., but I needed to recharge my laptop urgently and had difficulty finding an electric plug. Eventually I found one behind the curtain on the stage. I sat there quietly to get the basic charge, and was reading some journal papers to pass the time.

I heard some noise on the stage, and it was the second co-chair with at least three other people having an informal meeting using the chairs and table set up for the panel. They were speaking in my own language. Basically the co-chair was furious at being treated "rudely" by the other co-chair, and this group of senior people began to start plotting about reducing the rude person's influence on the project.

I kept totally silent while this plotting went on for about 20 minutes. Then the group left the stage.

What could I do? I was fairly certain if I told the "rude" co-chair, the whole project would have broken up in disarray and I would have lost out as a partner. If I confronted the plotters I might be accused of spying on them and it would probably have damaged my relationship with them, unless I chose to leverage my insider information in some way, which I was not interested in doing.

I discussed it with my co-researcher only, and we agreed to keep quiet about it all. There was hostility and anger at various points in the project between the co-chairs and others (I never knew exactly who all the plotters were). The project was completed successfully overall, though it wasn't much fun at times. We did several times counsel the rude co-chair to be careful about language in a project with so many cultures.

> On a few occasions my co-researcher and I were able to act as intermediaries to resolve some of the tensions. We were certainly very careful in our dealings with the plotters. Most noticeably, the rude co-chair got frozen out of leadership or even partnership of subsequent high-profile projects.

The narrative illustrates the tensions that can exist in group or team-based research. While the language of research may speak of "collaboration" there are frequently tensions between powerful, ambitious, or egoistic personalities that can come to the fore. At one level, it has never been easier to conduct research with international partners given the availability and affordability of the World Wide Web and airline travel. At another level, though, cultural differences between researchers from different countries are easy to underestimate despite the globalization of society. In this instance, my informant chose to remain quiet about what she had overheard. In deciding to take no direct action, the informant demonstrated the kind of tacit knowledge that researchers often possess. This was based, at least to some extent, on an evaluation of the "politics" of the situation including, possibly, a concern to ensure that they themselves did not challenge powerful parties in the research team. Some might consider this to be a somewhat spiritless failure to act but the informant clearly felt there was nothing to be gained for anyone from blowing the whistle on the "plotters." At the very least, it made the parties to this project appreciate the significant impact of respect for others and sensitivity to cultural differences in undertaking collaborative work.

A PERSONAL REFLECTION

This section of the book has included narratives generously contributed by a range of informants from different disciplines. It has sought to illustrate how they reflect on their own experiences as researchers and what lessons we can draw for understanding the role of virtue (and vice). The following narrative is a contribution of my own based on my early experiences as a researcher studying the attitudes of university lecturers in business and management education during the early 1990s.

Narrative 9.2

The Agreeable Interviewer

Some years ago I started interview-based research for a social science project. I developed a series of interview questions and also tape-recorded the interviews with the permission of the interviewees. At the time I was quite an inexperienced researcher.

One of the challenges I faced was trying to get my interviewees to relax and "open up" a bit more about their opinions. I discovered that it was a good idea to allow the interviewee to talk a little about themselves first as a way of relaxing them, gaining their trust, and generally "warming" them up. I was interested in their opinions on the topic being researched and so tended to nod encouragingly regardless of what they had to say. I remember reading that the technical term for this is "sanctioning" in that I was giving my implicit assent through appearing to agree with them. Sometimes, frankly, I could not have disagreed with them more but I found that I got a lot more out of the interviewee if I did signal my agreement through body language or saying something like "oh, I see what you mean" in a positive way. I guess this is also about me trying as best as I could to use my "emotional intelligence."

At the time, and since, I have thought about whether what I did was really right. I suppose that some of my gestures and comments might have been construed, strictly speaking, as misleading. On balance though I think what I did was okay. While I suppose there is a degree of deception in "sanctioning" it did help to encourage people to express their true beliefs.

If I had signaled my disapproval at certain points it might have led to people being much less frank or getting side-tracked into an argument with me. After all, the point of doing the interviews was to try to understand the different perspectives of the interviewees, however much one might personally agree or disagree with the opinions being expressed.

As a doctoral student in full-time employment before the advent of compulsory training, I received little formal preparation for my fieldwork. I relied mainly on interviewing my peers in other higher education institutions who were also business and management lecturers. One of my main concerns was a purely practical one in getting people to agree to be interviewed. While most of my interviewees were my "peers" they were mainly older and more senior academics working at other institutions. My interviewing "style" at this time reflected my status as a relatively lowly, young researcher often interviewing more experienced and senior lecturers. The inequality in the power relationship between me and my research interviewees meant that I felt impelled to demonstrate that I was on their "side." As a disciplinary peer, I felt a sense of comradeship with them and also an obligation to emotionally engage with their concerns and ideas. Their willingness to give up their time and contribute to my project meant that I felt a sense of mutual obligation. At the beginning of the interview, several interviewees asked what I had found out "so far." When asked this question I tended to avoid specifics or said that I would give them a short general summary at the conclusion of their interview as I was concerned not to influence what they would say in response to my questions. Hence, I was aware of the need to avoid influencing my interviewees at this point in the encounter.

Where I have subsequently used interviewing in my research I have sought to be careful to use less "sanctioning" behavior but have not changed my style substantially. One difference is that I have learnt to allow interviewees more "space" by asking fewer questions and allowing them to develop their answers in more depth. Transcribing my own interview tapes helped me to appreciate that I was often interjecting with another question just at the point at which the interviewee was pausing to think. While it is always tempting to "fill up" a pause, I have found that it is often better to allow the interviewee time to ponder or, if necessary, to prompt them to explain what they mean by something they have just said. This type of insight is nothing special and will often be recounted by any experienced interviewer. However, it serves as an example of what can be gained from the reflective process.

CONCLUSION

Reflexivity is an important intellectual and moral virtue for researchers to possess. It demands conscious engagement with the trials and tribulations of being a researcher through analyzing experiences. Without this virtue researchers are likely to struggle to develop their practice over time and can become more easily entrenched in dogmatic habits and particular methods of investigation. Ultimately, reflexivity is about wanting to improve and caring about trying to become a better researcher.

PART THREE

INTEGRATING INTEGRITY

The final section of the book will seek to place the virtues identified in the previous section in a broader context. My approach has been to consider the ethical challenges of being a researcher mainly from the perspective of the individual. However, the individual must operate within a societal framework which brings to bear pressures to perform in certain ways associated with their role. Researchers are also subject to formal education and training programs and more informal learning processes that help shape their understanding of research ethics. In short, we learn about research ethics from the example set by others. Finally, this section will conclude with a consideration of how the virtues of research intersect with the virtues connected with the broader academic role through teaching and service activities.

10

THE PERFORMATIVE CULTURE

The idea of *audit* has been exported from its original financial context to cover ever more detailed scrutiny of non-financial processes and systems. (O'Neil, 2002, 47)

INTRODUCTION

This book has attempted to sketch a portrait of the "virtuous" researcher. This is someone who tries to strike a balance between extremes of behavior and endeavors to stay true to their values in the process. They care about connecting their value set with their role as a researcher and seek to "live out" these virtues as best as they can in practice. The book has also presented to the reader a set of "virtues" associated with the process of research which is not specific to any one particular discipline or subject field. However, even assuming that these are the "right" virtues, the critic may point out that such expectations are easier to identify in theory than for individuals to put into practice. Part of the reality of this practice is the "performative" nature of contemporary academic life.

The earlier chapters of this book have made frequent, if passing, reference to the pressures which researchers face in the modern age. These include the pressures to gain external funding for their research, publish results in high-quality journals, and engage in a generally "competitive" way with others for finite resources in pursuing their work. It would be a mistake to assume that such pressures are something entirely new. Academic life has always been competitive although to the uninitiated it might give the outward appearance that it is not. It would probably be more accurate to assert that academic life is now even more competitive than it used to be. There is plenty of evidence to support this claim linked to the growth of government audit of research quality. Systems for auditing research are well established in the UK, Australia, Hong Kong, and New Zealand. The grand narrative that lies behind this regular auditing of the research "performance" of academics is a working culture based increasingly on "performativity." This chapter will explore the meaning of performativity in research and how this culture affects several of the virtues identified earlier in the book.

PERFORMATIVITY

We live in a less deferential age. Doctors, lawyers, teachers, engineers, and academics are no longer afforded automatic respect on the basis of their professional credentials.

In many respects, this decline of deference is a positive feature of modern life connected with higher levels of general education. However, this has also been accompanied by an apparent loss or crisis of "trust" in professionals (O'Neil, 2002). In an information-rich age, access to the internet means that the public no longer needs to take the professional's word for anything. A patient can check up on a doctor's diagnosis while a potential student or a concerned parent can check up on a university's ranking in a "league table." This loss of trust has been accompanied by a much expanded "audit" culture. Audit is a term most closely associated with financial scrutiny. However, it is now also commonly used to refer to the way that non-financial processes and procedures are scrutinized in public sector organizations to ensure that they are offering a good quality of (public) service.

The old systems by which quality was assured in public sector organizations have been stealthily displaced by new ones reliant more on managerial authority rather than peer control (Power, 1997). In UK universities, while external examiners still have formal authority, their role has been undermined in reality by the appearance of a more centralized system of quality control embodied by the Quality Assurance Agency for higher education (O'Neil, 2002). The growth of inspection regimes for educational provision in schools, further education colleges, and universities in the UK has increased the pressure to identify "measurable" outcomes for different types of academic activity (Avis, 2003). These measures are constructed as a means to gauge the impact of academic work on the enhancement of economic performance and efficiency. Similar trends can be found in the educational systems of other countries.

Performativity has been applied to the measurement of both teaching and research activity. Performativity in relation to teaching includes expectations or "targets" with respect to student completion rates, degree results, and employer satisfaction with graduates (Skelton, 2005). Increasingly, the lecturer is held directly accountable for the successful execution of these performative expectations. Teaching observation and course evaluation questionnaires completed by students are used to judge whether someone is a "good" teacher, on the basis largely of assumptions derived from the dramaturgical metaphor (Macfarlane, 2007b). Teaching that challenges students to think critically may not necessarily be considered "good" teaching if it fails to produce good examination results or immediately satisfied "customers."

In the same way that performative expectations have come to define the meaning of "good" teaching, "good" research is also being redefined by the culture of performativity. This means that individual researchers from a large number of disciplines are now being evaluated in terms of perceptions of the economic value of their research work. The "traditional rules" of research (Brew, 2001a) have always included pressures to publish but these are now accompanied by added expectations. For example, research councils and other grant-making bodies are placing increasing emphasis on assessing the "economic impact" of research, a requirement now extended to pure as well as applied work (Walker, 2007). Here, there is a risk that researchers will chase grant opportunities where they can demonstrate the short-term benefits of their research rather than focus on longer-term, theoretically driven work sometimes referred to as "blue skies thinking." Scientific breakthroughs are frequently preceded by 30 years or more of theoretical research particularly in "data-rich" disciplines such as chemistry or archaeology. In a world where the relatively short-term economic impact of funding for research is becoming a more significant consideration this has to be a cause for concern.

A recent review of health research funding in the UK appears to lend further weight to concerns about a creeping performative culture. The Cooksey Report (Cooksey, 2006) recommends increased emphasis on the "translation" of basic scientific research into the development of new products to treat illness and diseases. It also calls for a strengthening of knowledge and technology transfer between universities and businesses in the medical industries. The report, though, has been criticized for recommending the creation of an Office for Strategic Coordination of Health Research. This, according to evidence submitted to a Parliamentary committee by UK universities, may further bureaucratize administrative arrangements and possibly stifle blue skies research (House of Commons Science and Technology Committee, 2007). However, in the wake of the Cooksey Report, key funding bodies such as the UK Medical Research Council are placing more emphasis on goal-oriented research that is "translation-friendly." In the UK Research Assessment Exercise (RAE) of 2008, individual researchers across all disciplines were required to give evidence of the "impact" of their research published between 2001 and the end of the 2007 calendar year. Here, there is a risk that such a requirement may lead to a higher rating being awarded to a publication that has a short-term impact on shaping theoretical or applied knowledge in its field but a lower rating accorded to one that will have long-term impact but no immediate discernible effect.

Economic impact is just one dimension of performativity. There are many other dimensions illustrating the emphasis on audit, measurement, and the setting of targets. Another is rate of personal publication. Despite the collaborative nature of much research work, especially in the sciences, it is individuals who receive research grants or prestigious honors (Louis et al., 2007). It is also an individual who will be the first named author on a published paper or benefit from a promotion. Being classified as "research-active" is now essential to the career prospects of most UK academics. The tensions associated with who gets credit for publication, including the order in which names appear, were illustrated earlier in this book (see chapter 8). The history of academic enterprise is littered with examples of authorship disputes but performative pressures have exacerbated such tensions.

While superficially straightforward, the Research Assessment Exercise has resulted in a range of time-consuming and costly activities by universities in an attempt to maximize their funding. So called "submission strategies" (Talib and Steele, 2000) have led to the commitment of extra resources to secure a higher research rating (and hence funding) by, among other things, releasing key staff from teaching duties to produce additional publications and the recruiting (or "poaching") of research "stars" from other institutions. Most damaging of all, however, is the creation of a "them and us" attitude amongst staff (Harley, 2002). This has been created by dividing lecturers into those who are "research-active" and those who are not, with the result that the latter group feel threatened, marginalized, and inferior in status (Thomas, 2001).

Although slightly different in methodology, the Australian Research Quantum fulfills a similar function to the UK's RAE in determining research funding for universities. In this system, a Composite Index gives weightings to different types of publications such as edited books, refereed journal articles, or doctoral theses supervised to completion. The Composite Index acts as a blunt instrument that pays no regard to disciplinary differences in publication patterns. While since its introduction the Composite Index has been adjusted in the light of criticism, it still distorts the research output of staff under pressure to maximize institutional performance and commensurate funding. Again, the overall effect has been to elevate the importance of research productivity at the expense of teaching (Harman, 2000). While the election of a new government in Australia in late 2007 resulted in the scrapping of the Research Quantum Framework, a metrics-based system has been announced in its place that will bring other pressures to bear on Australian researchers (Rout and Knott, 2007).

As a result of audit exercises that privilege publication in refereed journals, other forms of publication are no longer considered to offer an equivalence of status. The pressure to publish in peer-reviewed journals in many subject areas has led to a loss of prestige for and interest in writing materials essential to teaching (Alderman, 2000). This has resulted in academic staff producing the "wrong sort" of research and publications, such as student textbooks or articles for applied or professional periodicals, being excluded from the selectivity process or pressurised into re-orientating their efforts towards peer-reviewed journals instead. Promotion prospects can be adversely affected by scholars who commit their careers to forms of publication or research in areas, such as the scholarship of teaching, that fall outside the conventional boundaries of the discipline (Attwood, 2007; Stierer, 2007). Those who seek to traverse such boundaries have to take an added risk in a performative culture where the rewards and honors are firmly attached to particular lines of enquiry and forms of productivity.

THE CITATION GAME

While government audit of research quality, based mainly on peer review processes, is a common method for allocating funding for university research, it is far from universal. A more internationally recognized means of making judgments about the reputation and prestige of an academic is in relation to the extent to which others cite his or her research in their own publications. For example, in contrast with the UK, assessment of research quality in the Netherlands has tended to use a combination of peer review processes and bibliometric data (Moed et al., 2004). The Science Citation Index (SCI), which dates back to 1964 and is now owned by Thomson Scientific (Moed, 2005), produces a quantitative measure of author citations in footnotes and bibliographies of many thousand journals worldwide. The SCI also enables one to identify which journals are the most frequently cited. The index has broadened its scope to include social sciences and the humanities but is still seen as providing a more comprehensive coverage of journals in the science and technology field (Moed, 2005). It has become increasingly influential as a means of determining the "impact" that an academic is having in their discipline, particularly in science and technology subjects, by reference to the number of times they have been cited. Citation is a proxy for the "influence" or "impact" of a researcher on the thinking of colleagues in their academic community.

Although based on peer review since it was introduced in 1986, there was an attempt to introduce metrics into the UK RAE in the early 1990s, but a joint consultation paper from the then Universities Funding Council and the Committee of Vice Chancellors and Principals met with fierce opposition from British academics critical of the citation method (Anderson, 1991). However, the tide has now turned against the cost and time-consuming nature of the current peer review system. In future, the UK government will rely more heavily on statistical information (or "metrics") in evaluating university research quality, such as that provided through SCI, rather than the more costly and time-consuming peer review system (HEFCE, 2007).

There are, though, well-known problems with the use of metrics and, perhaps ironically, the author who first suggested the development of the "impact factor" in evaluating academics by citation, Eugene Garfield (Smith, 2006), has identified a number of these problems himself. Firstly, it is a common practice for academics to cite their own previous publications. Often this is perfectly legitimate in helping the reader to understand how their current research links with previous work. Sometimes, however, excessive self-citation can occur. This is an example of a boastful practice in terms of the vices. Regardless of the motivation, self-citation can falsely inflate the ranking of an individual and any metric indicator needs to take account of the extent of such a practice (Garfield & Welljams-Dorof, 1992).

Another alleged behavioral effect of metrics is the formation of citation "rings" or "cartels." These are groups of academics who conspire to cite the work of each other in preference to other researchers (Garfield & Welljams-Dorof, 1992). Such a practice will tend to have an impact on the reliability of metric data. To some extent this type of practice is inevitable in tightly formed academic communities where it may come about naturally as a result of interaction over a number of years rather than as a deliberate conspiracy. It is the result of what is sometimes referred to as the "invisible college" or "network" (Halsey & Trow, 1971). Nonetheless, the effect is to exclude others who are not members of the inner circle of a particular academic community. According to some critics US authors tend to excessively cite the work of other US academics (Moed, 2005). This is a possible example of a citation ring on a larger scale and it is probable that elsewhere in the academic world citation practices will tend to be "skewed" towards national contexts. This is probably more about parochialism than xenophobia, although the effect can be discriminatory and leads to an under-representation of researchers from other countries or regions.

It is also dangerous to assume that being cited is necessarily an indicator of prestige. It may indicate quite the opposite where the ideas of a particular researcher or author are controversial or considered antiquated in some way. In the field of business ethics, the late Milton Friedman wrote an article for the *New York Times Magazine* in 1970 (Friedman, 1970) that subsequently became a target for sustained critique among academic business ethicists for rejecting the argument that business organizations had ethical obligations beyond maximizing the financial gains of their shareholders. In fact, such was the notoriety of Friedman's article that very few major academic papers about business ethics or corporate social responsibility have subsequently been published without challenging or at least citing it in passing (Hood, 1998). The frequent citations accorded to Friedman's article are not, therefore, an indicator of the esteem with which he is held in the field but indicate quite the opposite. This is an example of the way in which there tend to be more negative or critical citations in the social sciences than in the "hard" sciences where references are more usually positive (Garfield & Welljams-Dorof, 1992). What is even more worrying is that positive citation can continue to occur after a large number of papers have either been retracted or discredited by subsequent research (Smith, 2006).

Such is the importance of increasing the impact factor of a journal according to the SCI that journal editors have sought to persuade Thomson Scientific to reduce the number of articles that are deemed to qualify for citation (Smith, 2008). One of the effects of this kind of game-playing behavior is that a journal can become less "readable" for practitioners, such as general medical practitioners, as papers are limited to those reporting empirical findings rather than matters of debate or more general interest (Smith, 2008). Political machinations within editing and reviewing processes were noted earlier in the book (see chapter 8) where a narrative illustrated the potential for abuse of the power vested in referees when a paper contains references to the reviewer's own publications. Unscrupulous individuals may abuse their power by only agreeing to recommend a paper for publication if it includes such single or multiple citations to their previous research (Franck, 1999).

These are just some of the problems and criticisms attached to the use of metrics to determine the impact and standing of academic research. What is crucial to consider, however, is how the performative culture may have other, more general behavioral effects on researchers that might adversely affect their integrity. In terms of the virtues outlined in this book, many are in danger of being undermined by performative pressures. Some of these issues have already been highlighted in Part 2, but it is also important to briefly summarize these risks.

PERFORMATIVITY AND VIRTUE

The pressure for significant results can lead to corner-cutting behavior in gathering research data or performing experiments. An attitude of "results at all costs" may also lead to the mistreatment of research subjects or, possibly more commonly, doing the minimum necessary to ensure they are adequately informed. At the dissemination stage, results can be "salami-sliced" in order to produce several publications, rather than one long one. This type of behavior may be exacerbated by research quality audit exercises that place too much emphasis on the number of publications. Rate of publication does not necessarily result in "better" research. The number of publications produced has been used for several years as part of the formula for allocating government funding for university research in Australia. The effect of this criterion, though, has been to encourage greater publication without reference to the quality of this output (Butler, 2003).

Performative pressures place a strain on the virtue of humility in evaluating the significance of research. Narrative overviews of the work of researchers in successive RAE audit exercises in the UK have tended to encourage the use of boastful terminology or hyperbole to represent the extent to which academic work is "international," "influential," or "highly significant." There is also pressure on the writers of narrative overviews to exaggerate the extent of collaborative work with prestigious partners or the degree to which researchers work together in pursuing a common theme or line of enquiry, particularly in the humanities and social sciences, where individual research is more commonly found. At the same time, asking authors to estimate their individual contributions to joint publications provides a further dangerous temptation to exaggerate the truth. The broader impact of the performative culture may be found in boastful personal websites and exaggerated claims in curricula vitae.

As argued in chapter 4, courage is a virtue that sometimes demands going against the grain of popular trends or opinion to which, currently, little prestige or research income opportunities may attach. Research often entails questioning received wisdom and generating new or nuanced theories, concepts, and discoveries. The essential purpose of such research is often to challenge the *status quo*. This process need not be simply destructive of the existing knowledge base but may help to reconstruct our shared understanding of the nature of truth. The policy priorities of research granting bodies are increasingly shaped by a need to demonstrate responsiveness to shorter-term impact and currently popular themes. Areas of research can be unfashionable. In history, it is claimed that historians have "lost the big picture" partly as a result of the increasing specialization of historians into silos (Corfield, 2007, 14). As a result it is claimed that no one is writing "grand narratives" trying to explain the course of human history through integrating different social, economic, political, and cultural traditions. Some areas of scientific investigation, such as anatomical research, are similarly considered to be less popular or fast moving in nature than others such as molecular biology (Coleman, 1999).

CONCLUSION

The performative culture is symptomatic of a society in which there has been an erosion of trust in the professions and those working in the public sector, such as university academics. The effect of this has been to create a contemporary research environment that places a strain on many of the virtues essential to the ethical conduct of research as outlined in this book. This means that the role of the academic, particularly more senior or experienced faculty, is critical in resisting pressures that erode research integrity and passing on such attitudes to junior colleagues and graduate research students.

11

LEARNING ABOUT VIRTUE

Every good scholar and every good scientist who teaches research
methods can and should teach research ethics. (Pimple, 1995, 11)

INTRODUCTION

In this chapter, I will consider how a "virtue-based" approach may be
translated into the way that postgraduate research students are taught
and learn about research ethics. Currently, the teaching of research
ethics is still in its infancy, often included as a minor part of a research
methodology or induction course for postgraduate research students.
The chapter will critique common practices and approaches in the
teaching of research ethics in this context and make suggestions about
how a virtue-based approach can contribute to the development of
researchers. The analysis of current provision for research training in
ethics will identify the shortcomings of dominant approaches that are
often based on a discourse of compliance, an over-reliance on extreme
illustrations of "wrong-doing," and a theoretical base drawn from
prevalent principle-based theories rather than virtue ethics. The potential of an approach based on virtue theory will be presented as an
alternative means of developing researcher awareness and understanding of research ethics based on more fine-grained scenarios that engage
with the personal values of the learner.

THE EVOLVING CURRICULUM

It is now a common requirement for postgraduate research students to
have received some form of "ethics" education or training as part of

their formal development. In the USA, the National Institutes of Health requires that those students in receipt of federal funding should have received some form of formal research ethics education. Professional bodies that accredit courses in higher education institutions also have stipulations. Since the mid-1990s, for example, the Australian Psychological Association has required university professional training courses to contain a component that addresses ethical aspects of research and practice as part of its accreditation guidelines (Davidson et al., 2003). Psychological associations have broadly similar expectations in other national contexts. In the UK, the Quality Assurance Agency for higher education (QAA) code of practice on postgraduate research programs contains guidance on expectations with respect to developing student awareness of ethical issues (Quality Assurance Agency for higher education, 2004). In a joint statement with the UK research councils, appendix 3 of the code of practice contains details of the "skills training" requirements for research students.

> Demonstrate awareness of issues related to the rights of other researchers, of research subjects, and of others who may be affected by the research eg confidentiality, ethical issues, attribution, copyright, malpractice, ownership of data and the requirements of the Data Protection Act. (QAA, 2004, 34)

While the code is ostensibly a statement about "skills" it includes a number of injunctions that are essentially behavioral in nature. For example, in relation to the "skill" of personal effectiveness the code states that research students should have "flexibility and open-mindedness" and "be self-reliant." Under the heading of networking and teamworking it identifies an expectation that learners should "respond perceptively to others." Here, a number of attitudes and values are (mis)cast under the catch-all heading of "skills." By categorizing key dispositions in this way, bundling them together with technical skills such as the use of information technology, the code gives the impression that complex attitudinal dispositions are part of a simple linear process of skills development.

The code also states that institutions are required to provide students with their own university's research ethics standards and with the codes of other relevant professional bodies and discipline groups as part of any induction program. It stresses the importance of students being familiar with such documentation. However, the code is essentially silent on the key question of how to educate researchers to ensure that they are likely to comply with such expectations beyond drawing their attention to such documentation.

In interpreting the growing requirements of professional associations, funding bodies, and university authorities, research ethics has tended to be incorporated as a minor component within methodology courses across many subject areas. Yet, there are a number of assumptions and constraints that characterize the teaching of research ethics which I will outline in the section that follows.

ETHICS AS A CONSTRAINT

The teaching of research ethics often takes place in the context of a broader research methodology education or training program. Students from many disciplines can find such courses even more difficult and demanding than their own major subject studies (Murtonen & Lehtinen, 2003). Negative attitudes and difficulties in learning "quantitative" research methods are particularly apparent among students in the humanities and social sciences (Murtonen, 2005; Wisker et al., 2003). As a result, conventional coverage of "qualitative" and "quantitative" research methodologies, and accompanying design issues, may lead to the impression that there is little space to accommodate research ethics (Bryant & Morgan, 2007). Where space is found this can be primarily justified on the basis of a compliance approach. The teaching of research ethics is often conjoined with legal issues, such as the importance of researchers complying with the Data Protection Act or the relevant health and safety legislation in a UK context. While it is commonplace to conjoin the study of law and ethics there is a need to distinguish clearly between the two. In this context, the law demands understanding and compliance whereas ethics can help to shed a critical light on whether existing laws are good or bad and if we need to create new ones. Ethics is about thinking for oneself, not uncritical compliance.

Moreover, the teaching of "research ethics" can also be seen as an opportunity for universities to discharge their responsibilities to communicate details of their codes of research ethics to students. These considerations can lead to an approach to the teaching of research ethics consisting of little more than an explanation of the constraints to which researchers must conform. In a survey of the research ethics content of psychology courses accredited by the Australian Psychology Association, it was reported that "the most commonly used instructional approach involved teaching about the professional and research codes of ethics and ethical guidelines" (Davidson et al., 2003, 220). The "slavish attention" (Davidson et al., 2003, 220) that the ethics curriculum pays to such codes reinforces perceptions among learners that ethics is about compliance rather than developing a deep personal understanding of the values that underpins their own practice as an academic research scholar. It can reduce ethics to little more than gaining "ethical approval" for a project and demonstrating how to use a lexicon of concern about research "subjects" (see chapter 2).

ETHICS AND WRONG-DOING

The teaching of research ethics frequently focuses on examples of wrong-doing or malpractice rather than well-meaning attempts to do the right thing. Approaching the teaching of ethics in this way often involves the use of well-publicized examples of bad or unlawful behavior illustrated through case studies. Ethics teaching across a range of subject areas including medical, business, psychology, and research ethics deploy case studies that seek to illustrate real or real-to-life scenarios. While such cases can help students to understand the connections between theory and practice through discussion they invariably involve analyzing incidents of wrong-doing (e.g. Strohmetz & Skleder, 1992). Class demonstrations can also include getting students to reflect on the experience of being deceived as a research subject (Zhang & Moore, 2005). Textbooks in the field tend to reinforce the prevalence of studying malpractice or misconduct rather than good practice through their choice of cases and materials (e.g. Koocher and Keith-Spiegel, 1998; Penslar, 1995). Similarly, students can be asked to complete assignments that involve identifying what they believed to be the "unethical" manipulation of research subjects or some other form of "reprehensible" behavior (Rosnow, 1990).

Focusing on malpractice creates an impression that the practice environment is beset with often extreme versions of misconduct and can, inadvertently, suggest to students that such behavior represents the norm rather than the exception. It further means that while students may be able to understand what constitutes "unethical" practice they may find it harder to articulate the opposite and consider the values which might characterize "good" practice.

ETHICS AND THE CASE STUDY SCANDAL

Research students will probably have heard of relatively recent or infamous scandals. Examples include the Korean scientist, Woo Suk Hwang, who fraudulently claimed to have cloned an Afghan dog, the Tuskegee syphilis scandal, and the retention of the hearts of dead children at the Royal Liverpool Children's Hospital at Alder Hey.

Invariably, research ethics training will use these kinds of noteworthy incidents of research malpractice or abuse (Deming et al., 2007). Such high-profile illustrations of wrong-doing carry a tabloid newspaper value inasmuch as they are about individuals, or possibly research organizations in a dramatic fall from grace. They allow us all to stand back and condemn such blatant wrong-doing, often by those who were formerly trusted and held in high public esteem. However, such scandals are not easy for students to relate to at a personal level since they frequently involve experienced and famous scientists and multi-million pound research projects. They involve, in short, unfamiliar contexts beyond their personal experience. Moreover, the personal dilemmas and temptations that may have led to a decision to defraud or deceive may receive little real attention amid the more salacious or over-simplified headlines.

Research scandals involving inhuman treatment of human subjects or outright fraud are much more unusual than the everyday temptations and dilemmas faced by the ordinary researcher. Such scandals invariably fail to raise the sort of fine-grained issues that are likely to confront a possibly young and inexperienced lone researcher carrying out their first substantive academic investigation. These may involve lone, personal decisions unlikely to ever reach the attention of others, such as whether to under-report data that contradicts a hypothesis or not to completely fulfill promises to research subjects about letting them see interview transcripts or a subsequent published paper. Here, the human vice of laziness may be as relevant as any intent to defraud or mislead (see chapter 6). While such issues may be less dramatic they are also likely to be more real to the experiences of novice, or even more seasoned, researchers.

ETHICS IS ABOUT "SOLVING" DILEMMAS

When courses on research ethics do venture into the teaching of philosophy and moral theory they may do so in a predictably conventional way through utilitarianism, Kantianism, and rights theory. These theories form the basis of the bioethical principles found in most research codes (Beauchamp & Childress, 1979). Courses in other fields of professional and applied ethics are similarly dominated by principle-based theories. The teaching of business ethics, for example, also draws largely on utilitarianism, Kantianism, and rights theory (Macfarlane & Ottewill, 2001). This offers students a range of theories upon which to base their decisions when responding to case study dilemmas.

However, such a mix of principles can result in an "à la carte" interpretation of ethics: simply cherry-picking parts of theories that justify decisions. In some situations, one might apply a utilitarian rationale to justify research studies involving suffering to animals that promise benefits in advancing a cure for a particular cancer. In another situation one might fall back on a Kantian analysis by asserting that the mistreatment of research subjects can never be justified on the basis of the principle of reversibility. Applied to particular situations, the range of principles of research ethics adopted by most professional and other organizational bodies can be ambiguous and contradictory (Fisher & Kuther, 1997). Step-by-step decision-making models carry the biggest dangers. Firstly, such approaches take elements of utilitarianism and Kantianism in a way that legitimizes an "à la carte" approach. This might include a "stage" that considers the ill-effects on research subjects, from a Kantian perspective, and then another that requires someone to balance the costs and the benefits of undertaking an experiment, from a utilitarian standpoint. Secondly, such an approach effectively places the values of the individual *outside* of the decision-making process by reducing ethics to a formula. This falsely suggests that such decisions are pain-free and that cold analysis may remove any personal self-doubt.

In fighting for space and legitimacy within the academic curriculum, courses in ethics, including those concerning research, often emphasize that they help to develop students with improved powers of analysis, thus minimizing uncertainty and strengthening decision-making. The development of analytical skills and reducing ambiguity are two of the general goals in the teaching of ethics in higher education (Callahan, 1980). This appeals to the convention that academic knowledge should be logical and analytical while also suggesting that there is an instrumental rationale to ethics education.

ETHICS IS "TOO DIFFICULT" TO TEACH

For some tutors of research methods, the requirement to include an "ethics" component is an unwelcome addition to an already crowded curriculum (Bryant & Morgan, 2007; Swazey & Bird, 1997). The relative importance and status attached to research ethics is often betrayed by its position in the taught curriculum: as an afterthought appearing as one of the final taught elements. Placing research ethics at the tail-end of the curriculum provides a clear signal of its relative importance to the student body. It is something that "has" to be included but only to satisfy the formal course requirements. The relative status of research ethics within research methodology courses and perceptions that it is "difficult" to teach can lead to this work being sub-contracted to other tutors in biosciences, law, philosophy, or theology who may either specialize in the teaching of ethics or are interested in such issues that occur in their discipline. In a survey of university bioscience lecturers in the UK, just 33% felt that a biologist was adequately equipped to engage students with ethical theory and issues (Bryant & Morgan, 2007). This is partly due to an understandable lack of confidence in teaching a course that includes elements of moral philosophy.

Unfortunately, though, where the "main" tutor on a research training program gives over responsibility for research ethics to someone outside their subject field this can be perceived from a student perspective as a subtle, if possibly unintentional, signal that research ethics is not a mainstream concern for the discipline. Moreover, it is important that those teaching research ethics understand the context and the situational complexity, in the same way that business ethics needs to be taught by those that know business, rather than being left to philosophers and theologians (Chesley & Anderson, 2003). Anyone who teaches research methods should have the responsibility, and the capacity, to teach research ethics as an integral part of their course rather than something which they would rather hive off to someone else (Pimple, 1995).

LEARNING VIRTUE

While academics may feel uncomfortable or ill-equipped to teach research ethics on a formal basis they still inculcate key attitudes and values in their research students through the supervision process. Most academics learn about the ethical dimensions of research through their "apprenticeship" as doctoral students rather than as a result of formal training programs. In this respect, doctoral supervisors are significant role models in the process of socializing new researchers (Louis et al., 2007; Mendoza, 2007). They are the primary socializing agents who help to shape the values and norms of the next generation of researchers. The observation of good examples or behaviors, whether knowingly or unknowingly set by role models, is the basis for learning virtue (Ryle, 1972). Similarly, bad examples can inculcate vice. The socialization process is critical in shaping the values that will come to define the future leadership of academic disciplines.

Scientists tend to be socialized as part of research teams, the size of which can have an impact on the absorption of certain values. Tensions can exist in research teams where equitable opportunities to give everyone the opportunity to practice the full range of investigatory, analytical, and reporting skills in academic work may be at odds with the object of getting work done efficiently, resulting in the publication of results (Louis et al., 2007). These tensions can be more attenuated in larger groups where the division of labour will normally be greater. Research assistants may need to compete for attention with the more senior academic staff and to be included in jointly authored papers. At a more fundamental level, newer researchers will learn operating values, such as the extent to which research teams are open about sharing results with the wider academic or scientific community as opposed to maintaining secrecy to meet the demands of commercial sponsorship or to secure a patent. The importance of sincerity will be learnt through the attention of a supervisor to the detail of accuracy and truthfulness in their approach to research methods. In the natural sciences there may be a particularly strong emphasis on repeating experiments and demonstrating that a process is reproducible. This is about learning a virtue as much as a technical requirement.

USING VIRTUE

In response to the criticisms of existing approaches in the teaching of research ethics outlined above, there are a number of ways that virtue theory may aid researcher development. Firstly, as a theoretical perspective, virtue does not offer any ready-made solutions. It demands that researchers examine who they are and what they believe in rather than prescribing a course of action through the application of depersonalized principles. It can be argued that this restriction demonstrates the weakness of virtue theory since it offers an orientation to *being* rather than *doing*. However, this difference is also its strength in relation to principle-based theories since it demands that students engage personally with their own values and sense of what is right or wrong. While sets of virtues (and vices) drawn from Aristotle, Aquinas, Pring, and others contained in this book may be offered to students as a starting point, they are not intended to be prescriptive accounts of the only virtues or of those held by any one individual. In this way, students must draw on their own experiences, reflections, and resources to consider which virtues have resonance for them in relation to their own value set and in the context of their research. Virtue theory can help to empower students to connect their sense of who they *are* (as people) with what they are *doing* (as researchers). Another advantage of using virtue theory is that it is not normally perceived as a "difficult" theory to understand in comparison with more theoretically sophisticated interpretations of utilitarianism or Kantianism (van Hooft, 2006).

As an antidote to the conventional dependence of research ethics courses on scandal and misconduct, a virtue-based approach may identify individuals who represent the excellences of character valued by students as researchers. This approach has been successfully used in the context of the teaching of business ethics (Weber, 1995). Such an exercise does not need to take place in a critical vacuum, though, as clearly any such analysis needs to consider the character flaws and temptations that face any researcher. While such an exercise might focus on "famous" researchers it would be preferable to focus on "ordinary" researchers as represented in the narratives contained in this book. These narratives demonstrate the struggles of "ordinary" researchers to navigate the everyday ethical terrain of research. They rarely present extreme instances of wrong-doing but, rather, they offer fine-grained scenarios based on personal interpretation of virtue and vice within a particular disciplinary context. They are not intended as blueprints for "ethical" practice; nor are they devoid of well-meaning attempts to do the right thing. Individual students might be encouraged to record and analyze their own struggles to make what they feel is the right decision. Rather than relying on case studies about the experiences of others, students can be encouraged to write creatively about their own experiences or to develop outline stories further by considering the role of context, character, and plot (Atkinson, 2008).

The results of such narrative reflections do not necessarily confer on researchers superior "analytical" skills, but it may mean that as a result of studying research ethics they have been able to reflect critically about the implications of bringing their own set of values to the research arena. This is connected to developing practical wisdom as an Aristotelian virtue rather than becoming a dispassionate, cold-hearted analyst. A recent study has demonstrated that researchers use either practical wisdom or formal guidelines as a real means to make reasoned decisions (Deming et al., 2007). Only the former involves engaging with and connecting personal values with the research process and this is something that the teaching of research ethics needs to actively foster.

USING NARRATIVES

It is sometimes assumed that the teaching of ethics involves "preaching" to students about right and wrong or imposing the teacher's own moral views (Bryant & Morgan, 2007; Macklin, 1980). Adopting a virtue-based approach might be assumed to be more likely to entail "preaching" about a particular set of values or virtues. In fact, it affords an opportunity to interrogate such assumptions. Adopting a proselytizing approach is unlikely to be effective in getting students to engage with virtues that relate to their own experience or dispositions. In this respect, the teaching of research ethics needs to be approached in the same way as teaching any other academic discipline. In other words, it demands the critical interrogation of theoretical and personal perspectives rather than promulgating a particular set of values or opinions. This does not rule out a consideration of theories such as utilitarianism or Kantian, but the philosophical traditions they represent should not be given a privileged position in the curriculum.

Unlike principle-based moral theories, virtue ethics takes account of human desires and emotions from a "common sense" perspective (van Hooft, 2006). Virtue theory is not theoretical in the same way as Kantianism or utilitarianism. Nor does it rely on metaphysical dogma or doctrine. As such it provides a basis for teaching ethics, especially in a multi-cultural context, that is most likely to cut across differences based on culture, ideology, or religion.

CONCLUSION

Few researchers have been exposed to much in the way of formal research ethics education or training. Where this has occurred it has been mainly as an add-on to existing provision in methodological training or a dissemination of university guidelines. However, this does not mean that students have not learnt about the values and attitudes central to good research practice in their discipline through working with and observing the examples set by their peers and, especially, their research supervisors or leaders. It is important, though, for research ethics development to become more than an afterthought in the graduate student curriculum and for space to be found for discussion of values and fine-grained issues. In considering the virtues that are connected with the research process many are likely to connect with other aspects of the academic role, as a teacher, and in serving the community. How these virtues interrelate will form the subject of the final chapter.

12

THE GOOD PROFESSOR

Professional identity does not come ready-made. It involves a struggle for authenticity and, as such, has to be constructed. (Nixon, 2006, 159)

INTRODUCTION

The book has focused on discussing the moral virtues (and vices) associated with the research process. It has not considered, thus far, why academics ought to *do* research in the first place. Why, in other words, is research a moral imperative for academics? Such an imperative might appear to be a "given" to some academics who regard doing research as integral to their sense of identity and way of life. Others contend that research is essential to their academic freedom. Indeed, the right to conduct research and disseminate the results of such work was first asserted by the American Association of University Professors (AAUP) in its Statement of Principles on Academic Freedom and Tenure in 1940 (AAUP, 2008). However, the history of the university demonstrates that academics have not always been researchers. Rather, the notion of the university as a research body only began to take hold in Germany in the early nineteenth century and slowly spread elsewhere (Smith, 1999). In more modern times, there has been a trend toward the separation and "unbundling" (Kinser, 1998) of research from other elements of the academic role. Here, specialist positions such as teacher, instructional designer, and research professor are replacing that of the traditional, "all-round" academic.

In the book I have tended to consider the research role in isolation from the other core elements of the academic job description. Academics are also teachers and perform a range of service activities for the benefit of the university and its wider communities. The virtues associated with these other roles have been the subject of two of my previous books (Macfarlane, 2004, 2007a). Clearly, though, there are links and overlaps between the virtues of research, teaching, and service or "academic citizenship," as I and others refer to such activities (Macfarlane 2007a, Shils 1997, Thompson et al., 2005). In this final chapter I will firstly outline why engaging in research is a moral imperative for the academic and then go on to discuss how the virtues associated with research are linked to the two other principal elements of their role in teaching and service.

THE MORAL IMPERATIVE

Considerable debate currently surrounds the relationship between teaching and research. This debate focuses, in part, on how linking these two elements of the professorial role can make someone a more effective teacher. Recommendations include getting students to learn about research findings, how to do research themselves, and approaching their studies, at undergraduate and postgraduate level, in an enquiry-based mode (Healey & Jenkins, 2005). However, what is more rarely considered is why being a researcher is a moral responsibility for an academic beyond the practical ability to make someone into a better or more effective teacher. It is an academic duty as much as an academic freedom (Kennedy, 1997).

Perhaps the most obvious, immediate reason why an academic should do research is that for most faculty working within university contexts it is a part of their contractual obligation. This legal responsibility is rarely defined in much detail in academic contracts, though, beyond vague references to conducting research and scholarship. Often terms such as "scholarship" are left undefined and it is unusual to have specific requirements attached to contracts which indicate precise annual expectations in terms of individual targets for research grants or published articles, although a junior academic seeking tenure, or even a more senior academic or full professor, may have a clearer set of goals linked to performance review. Some academics do see doing research as an academic duty and fulfilling the requirements of the job description (Åkerlind, 2008). A range of often negative emotions may prevail, associated with keeping one's job and position rather than more positively setting out to discover. In some contexts, considerable emphasis is placed on research productivity as part of an initial "hurdle" to obtain a permanent or tenured academic position. Here, there is a risk that such expectations create a post-tenure culture that leads to some academics failing to sustain their commitment to scholarship, especially where performance requirements cannot subsequently be enforced. There may be more emphasis on doing research in a research-led university than in a higher education institution with a stronger orientation to teaching at a tertiary level. But this should not be interpreted to mean that academics working in more teaching-focused institutions are not equally committed to academic enquiry and often persevere as researchers despite limited opportunity or encouragement. Clearly, as this example illustrates, research is more than a contractual obligation. It is something that academics feel impelled to do. Part of this motivation has a moral element.

In understanding why academics should do research there is a clear link to their responsibility as teachers. One of the distinctive characteristics of a "higher" education is the opportunity for students to learn critically about propositional and professional knowledge (Barnett, 1990). This implies a broad definition of research across pure and more practice-based subjects. University education is about more than "learning more" about a given subject. It is about interrogating knowledge claims and being exposed to the latest thinking and research findings. This feature of higher education can only be supported in practice if academics are engaging in research which, in turn, informs their own teaching. Otherwise, universities will become little more than a finishing school for knowledge accumulation rather than an intellectually stimulating environment in which to debate, discuss, and challenge received wisdom. Students in higher education deserve to learn about the latest thinking and enjoy an environment where such knowledge, and the doubts associated with it, are shared. Academics not only need to stay up to date with their subject field but must also seek to continue to contribute to academic or professional research in order to be able to share these insights with their students. Being a researcher, or a current practitioner in a professional field, makes a university teacher *credible* beyond formal qualifications that may have been attained many years previously. While knowledge derived from research does not automatically make them a skillful teacher it is an essential precondition for teaching at a "higher" education level.

The experience of engaging in research activity also reminds academics what it is like to cope with the challenges of being a student again and to find their way through the challenging process of trying to learn more about the world. It is a process that keeps the academic "grounded" or in touch with what it is like to feel uncertain about one's own understanding about knowledge claims. Research is the only way to make higher education teaching an intellectually sustainable activity. Without research, teaching materials and the perspective of the professor will become increasingly dated and reliant, at best, on second-hand rather than primary insights into the latest thinking in a particular discipline or professional field.

Aside from responsibility for students, being a researcher is also important in making it possible for academics to have the capacity to fulfill their service commitments to other communities. These include their own institution, their discipline, or profession and the wider public (Macfarlane, 2007a). Academics gain their sense of identity from their discipline or allied profession (Becher & Trowler, 2001). This identity brings with it a responsibility to make a contribution both as a teacher and as a researcher. As a result, academics often see themselves as part of an intellectual tradition responsible for making a contribution to the accumulation, interrogation, and progression of knowledge in their field. Arguably, deciding not to make such a contribution is to take a "free ride" from one's own academic or intellectual peers (Corlett, 2005). It also means that academics are not in such a strong position to make a service contribution either to their own university or to the wider public.

Service contributions to academic institutions are often falsely portrayed as involving tedious, non-intellectual administrative tasks and, worse still, as either a rite of passage for young faculty or the (dead) end point of an academic career. In reality, most roles demand some form of applied scholarly expertise particularly in leading and managing colleagues from one's own discipline or profession or participating in initiatives and projects for the benefit of the university. Nearly all academics have the capacity to apply their specialist, research-based knowledge for the benefit of their institution. As an organization, a university needs good advice about many things: devising educational objectives; the effective management of people and resources; safeguarding the health and well-being of employees; understanding the organization's legal responsibilities; communicating with the media; planning environmental policies or architectural projects; and engaging purposefully in international relations, to name but a few examples. The capacity to provide this type of advice often lies within the walls of a university from its own professoriate. Too few institutions make sufficient use of this in-house expertise. Some faculty, such as educational developers, have an explicitly dual role, as both researchers in their discipline and service providers utilizing their expertise within the university. Yet, it needs to be understood that the credibility of those contributing to institutional or "mission-based" research can only be gained through their work as independent, specialist scholars with a reputation for the quality of their work beyond the walls of the university.

A researcher can share their expertise with the wider world, becoming an academic or scholarly citizen by deploying that knowledge for the common good. Here, academics may contribute to expert forums, government bodies and commissions, non-profit making and other non-governmental organizations, and public debates in executing this role. Moreover, communicating with the public on the basis of research expertise is not a possibility only limited to researchers in applied fields. Those working in "pure" disciplines also have a duty to seek to improve public understanding of the significance of their research to the daily lives of citizens. Maintaining public support and enthusiasm for particular academic disciplines entails working with schools, charitable bodies, and the media. Seeking to reach a wider audience for specialist research is, in this way, an important element of the implicit deal or "compact" between academics and society (Macfarlane, 2007a; National Committee of Inquiry into Higher Education, 1997). Åkerlind's research (2008) demonstrates that for some academics being a higher education researcher is very closely associated with advancing social change. For these academics their personal ideology and values are tied in with addressing research areas, such as environmentalism or racism, that are critical to the future well-being of society.

INTEGRATING INTEGRITY

Research is much more than a self-regarding individual activity. It is about becoming a fully fledged "academic citizen," someone who is prepared to and capable of contributing scholarly expertise for the benefit of others (Macfarlane, 2007a; Shils, 1997). This means that research is closely related to the service role of an academic. It is not an activity isolated from teaching or service although all too often this perception is reinforced both by the way governments separate funding for university teaching from research and by the way institutions operate internal performance systems that apply to academic faculty. Universities frequently compound this false bifurcation by branding themselves as "research-led" or "teaching-focused" institutions. There are, however, a lot of overlaps between the virtues that apply in respect to being a "good" researcher and these other aspects of the academic job that I have outlined in previous publications (Macfarlane, 2004, 2007a).

There are several virtues common to the roles of teacher, researcher

Table 12.1
The Virtues of Academic Practice

Teaching	Respectfulness, sensitivity, pride, courage, fairness, openness, restraint, collegiality
Service/Academic citizenship	Benevolence, collegiality, loyalty, guardianship, engagement
Research	Courage, respectfulness, resoluteness, sincerity, humility, reflexivity

Macfarlane (2004, 2007a)

and being an academic citizen (see Table 12.1). Courage is needed as a teacher to take appropriately calculated risks to innovate for the benefit of students. Here, it is easy to fall back into a comfort zone of tried and tested techniques that provide little or no challenge in extending one's own teaching expertise. In this context, more active approaches to student learning can demand courage on the part of the teacher to relinquish the control and "comfort" associated with their conventional role as an authority figure. Courage is also required, of course, as a researcher to set appropriately demanding questions, problems, or hypotheses, among other things (see chapter 4). Respectfulness to students is a critical part of being a good teacher in forming appropriate learning relationships and, as a researcher, it is essential in ensuring that human research subjects are treated with dignity (see chapter 5). Openness as a virtue in teaching can be compared with reflexivity in research.

These virtues are about maintaining a reflectively self-critical attitude that is vital both, in a teacher, in understanding and responding to student feedback and, in a researcher, in ensuring that we act upon an evaluation of our own strengths and weaknesses and the extent to which the research has fulfilled its original aims. Good teachers have always reflected on what they do and amended their practice accordingly. Similarly, a good researcher will not progress in their work without critically evaluating the extent to which they have achieved their own objectives.

Sincerity in research and restraint in teaching are critical moral virtues that have parallels but also subtle differences. The first of these virtues implies always seeking to be as truthful and accurate as possible as a researcher while "restraint" refers to the need for a teacher to be honest in communicating with students but to restrain themselves from an aggressive advocacy of a particular theoretical position or political stance. Here, the key difference is that a researcher is communicating largely with their peers who can engage on an equal basis in analysis and critique. A teacher, on the other hand, will be working with students, rather than peers. Adopting a proselytizing attitude in this context may undermine the self-confidence of students and the practical extent to which they will develop their own academic freedom or "voice" as a result. It may further be noted that collegiality appears as a virtue in teaching and in service but not in research. This might appear to be a curious omission. However, while working collaboratively with colleagues is an essential precondition for being a teacher and in contributing to the development of others through service, especially in some disciplines within the arts, humanities, and social sciences, it is quite possible to be a good researcher and remain a "lone ranger" rather than collaborate with others.

Turning to service or academic citizenship, here there are other virtues which are closely related to research. Guardianship is a virtue connected with responsibilities that result from being a more experienced researcher, such as reviewing manuscripts or grant submissions, editing the work of other scholars, and organizing conferences and events for the growth and benefit of research communities. It is vital that researchers do not abdicate from these responsibilities in the same way that commitment to institutional self-governance has begun to wither (Thompson et al., 2005). Guardianship is about upholding standards and subjecting the research ideas and results of others to critical judgment. It is not, however, about "gatekeeping" in the sense of blocking the development of new ideas, lines of thought, and individuals associated with particular theoretical or political stances with whom one might not agree. Rather, guardianship should entail positively encouraging and supporting others, particularly in regard to their research development. Collegiality and engagement are other virtues important to academic citizenship that call for a similar mind-set and closely relate to research support. Collegiality can entail acting as a research mentor to less experienced colleagues while engagement with a wider public audience is important in debating and explaining the application of one's discipline and its relevance to the lives of all members of society.

The close connections between the virtues of teaching, service, and research demonstrate how important each role is to being "an academic." It is also illustrative of the integrative, holistic nature of "integrity," as derived from its original Latin root. While there is now a trend to "unbundle" the academic role by creating specialist positions within universities for teachers, instructional designers, student counsellors, manager-academics, and researchers, this is motivated by economic forces rather than by the logic and integrative nature of academic practice. A teacher with no research interests cannot hope to pass on the excitement involved in the process of academic enquiry and will never be a fully fledged member of "their" own discipline. A researcher who has no teaching responsibilities is similarly more limited in their opportunity to disseminate new knowledge, understand emerging issues, or help shape the next generation of scholars in their field. Finally, someone who does not engage with service activities misses further opportunities to influence public understanding of their discipline or contribute to, and learn from, the scholarly development of others.

Academic identity is about a "struggle for authenticity" (Nixon, 2006, 159). Throughout the course of an academic career, this identity is being constructed and often reconstructed. This struggle means that academics are striving to become better, or more authentic, teachers, researchers, and academic citizens. These roles are interlocked, and retaining a commitment to perform each to the maximum of one's ability is part of what it means to be an academic.

CONCLUSION

At the beginning of the book, I outlined how the emphasis we have today on the rights of research subjects has its roots in post-war reaction to Nazi experimentation on Jews and other persecuted groups. Post-war reaction to these crimes against humanity led to the establishment of principles designed to eradicate the exploitation of research subjects. More recently, the erosion of trust in professionals and increasing managerial audit of public services have led to a situation where codification has sought to further prescribe and control research activities through bureaucratic approval procedures.

I have sought to demonstrate that research ethics is a complex subject that demands an active and continuing struggle with personal conscience. Practice needs to evolve in order to respond flexibly to particular situations. It is a complexity that demands engagement rather than disengagement with moral decision-making on the basis that we have obtained "ethical approval" or have a "code of practice" somewhere in our office. I have argued against an overly formalistic approach to research ethics that substitutes codification for a personal sense of responsibility characterized by virtues. No code can capture the day-to-day tensions that are part and parcel of the research process or conflicts connected with a researcher's personal stance. This involves deciding what *stance* to take in balancing a myriad of conflicting moral imperatives: whether to approach research as a "subjective" or "object-ive" activity; how to balance respect for research subjects with the desire to pursue the truth; or whether to adopt or challenge the stylistic conventions of one's discipline in the search for authenticity of expression. Even if a researcher claims not to take an open stance on such issues they do so implicitly through their actions, although the tensions that they need to manage are largely fine-grained in nature rather than dramatic or sensational.

One of the excuses put forward by the doctors at Nuremberg was that they were only "following orders." They contended, in effect, that they were bound by the rules that governed their activities. The inadequacy of this excuse was dismissed at the trial, as should the protestations of a researcher that their actions were only undertaken on the basis of the instructions of others or a set of guidelines. We are responsible for our own actions and need to connect with the virtues that (hopefully) guide us. It is only by maintaining and constantly developing an understanding of our own sense of integrity, and being critically aware of our own frailties, that we can hope to exercise the responsibilities of being a good researcher.

REFERENCES

Adler, F. (1918). *An ethical philosophy of life: Presented in its main outlines.* New York: D. Appleton & Company.

Akabayashi, A. & Slingsby, B.T. (2003). Biomedical ethics in Japan: The second stage. *Cambridge Quarterly of Healthcare Ethics,* 12, 261–264.

Åkerlind, G.S. (2008). An academic perspective on research and being a researcher: An integration of the literature. *Studies in Higher Education,* 33, 1, 17–31.

Alderman, G. (2000). Teaching and research in higher education. *Reflections on Higher Education,* 11, 26–34.

Alderman, H. (1997). By virtue of a virtue. In D. Statman (Ed.), *Virtue Theory: A Critical Reader* (pp. 145–164). Edinburgh, UK: Edinburgh University Press.

American Anthropological Association. (1998). *Code of Ethics of the American Anthropological Association,* http://www.aaanet.org/committees/ethics/ethcode.htm (accessed on August 8, 2006).

American Association of University Professors (AAUP). (2008). *1940 Statement of Principles on Academic Freedom and Tenure,* http://www.aaup.org/AAUP/pubsres/policydocs/contents/1940statement.htm (accessed on February 13, 2008).

American Psychological Association. (2002). *Ethical Principles of Psychologists and Code of Conduct,* http://www.apa.org/ethics/code2002.pdf (accessed on May 31, 2006).

Anderson, A. (1991). No citation analyses please, we're British. *Science,* 252, 639.

Anscombe, G.E.M. (1958). Modern moral philosophy. *Philosophy,* 33, 1, 1–19.

Aristotle. (1906). *The Ethics of Aristotle: The Nicomachean Ethics,* trans. G.H. Lewes, London: Walter Scott.

Ashby, E. (1967). Anatomy of the academic life. *Educational Record*, Winter, 48, 45–50.

Atherton, J.S. (2003). *Doceo: Learning as Loss1*, http://www.doceo.co.uk/original/learnloss_1.htm (accessed on December 3, 2007).

Atkinson, T.N. (2008). Using creative writing techniques to enhance the case study method in research integrity and ethics courses. *Journal of Academic Ethics*, 6, 33–50.

Attwood, R. (2007). Professor says teaching focus blocked career. *The Times Higher Education Supplement*, August 10.

Avis, J. (2003). Re-thinking trust in a performative culture: The case of education. *Journal of Education Policy*, 18, 315–332.

Baird, P. (2003). Getting it right: Industry sponsorship and medical research. *Canadian Medical Association Journal*, 168, 1267–1269.

Barnes, D.E. & Bero, L.A. (1998). Why review articles on the health effects of passive smoking research different conclusions. *Journal of the American Medical Association*, 279, 1566–1570.

Barnett, R. (1990). *The idea of a higher education*, Buckingham, UK: The Society for Research into Higher Education/Open University Press.

Barnett, R. (2007). *A will to learn: Being a student in an age of uncertainty*. Maidenhead, UK: The Society for Research into Higher Education/Open University Press.

Beauchamp, T. & Childress, J. (1979). (1st ed.) *Principles of biomedical ethics*. Oxford, UK: Oxford University Press.

Beauchamp, T. & Childress, J. (1989). (3rd ed.) *Principles of biomedical ethics*. Oxford, UK: Oxford University Press.

Becher, T. & Trowler, P. (2001). *Academic tribes and territories: Intellectual enquiry and the cultures of disciplines* (2nd ed.). Buckingham, UK: The Society for Research into Higher Education/Open University Press.

Benatar, S.R. (2002). Reflections and recommendations on research ethics in developing countries. *Social Science and Medicine*, 54, 7, 1131–1141.

Bennett, J. (1994). The Conscience of Huckleberry Finn. In *Ethics*, ed. P. Singer, 294–305. Oxford, UK: Oxford University Press.

Berger, P.L. & Luckmann, T. (1966). *The social construction of reality*. London: Penguin.

Beynon, H. (1977). *Working for Ford*. Harmondsworth, UK: Penguin.

Biotechnology and Biological Sciences Research Council. (2007). *BBSRC research grants: The Guide, version 7.0*, http://bbsrc.ac.uk/funding/apply/grants_guide.pdf (accessed December 8, 2007).

Blackmore, J. (2007). Is it only "what works" that "counts" in new knowledge economies? Evidence based practice, educational research and teacher education in Australia. *Social Policy and Society*, 1, 3, 257–266.

Blair, T. (2002). Statement to the House of Commons, 24 September, *Parliamentary Debates*, Commons, 6th Series, Vol. 390, (2001–2002), col. 3.

Bok, D. (2003). *Universities in the marketplace: The commercialisation of higher education*. Princeton, NJ: Princeton University Press.

Bourdieu, P. (1988). *Homo academicus*, trans. P. Collier. Stanford, CA: Stanford University Press.

Brew, A. (2001a). *The nature of research: Inquiry in academic contexts*. London: RoutledgeFalmer.

Brew, A. (2001b). Conception of research: A phenomenographic study. *Studies in Higher Education*, 26, 271–285.

British Broadcasting Corporation (BBC). (2004). *The Neil Report: Statement by the Board of Governors* (Chair: Ronald Neil). London: BBC, http://www.bbc.co.uk/info/policies (accessed on January 3, 2007).

Brockbank, A. & McGill, I. (1998). *Facilitating Reflective Learning in Higher Education*, Buckingham, UK: The Society for Research into Higher Education/Open University Press.

Bryant, J.A. & Morgan, C.L. (2007). Attitudes to teaching ethics to bioscience students: An interview-based study comparing British and American university teachers. *Bioscience Education Journal*, 9, http://www.bioscience.heacademy.ac.uk/journal/vol9/beej-9.3.pdf (accessed January 14 2008)

Butler, L. (2003). Modifying publication practices in response to funding formulas. *Research Evaluation*, 12, 1, 39–46

Callahan, D. (1980). Goals in the teaching of ethics. In D. Callahan and S. Bok (Eds.), *Ethics Teaching in Higher Education*. (pp. 61–80)., New York: Pelum Press.

Calvey, D. (2000). Getting on the door and staying there: A covert participant observational study of bouncers. In G. Lee-Treweek and S. Linkogle (Eds.), *Danger in the field: Risk and ethics in social research* (pp. 43–60). London: Routledge.

Cawley, M.J., Martin, J.E. & Johnson, J.A. (2000). A virtues approach to personality. *Personality and Individual Differences*, 28, 997–1013.

Chesley, G.R. & Anderson, B. (2003). Are university professors qualified to teach ethics?. *Journal of Academic Ethics*, 1, 2, 217–219.

Clegg, S. (2007). The possibilities of sustaining critical intellectual work under regimes of evidence, audit, and ethical governance. *Journal of Curriculum Theorizing*, 23, 2, 27–44.

Coleman, R. (1999). Impact factors: Use and abuse in biomedical research. *The Anatomical Record*, 257, 2, 54–57.

Collinson, J.A. (2005). Artistry and analysis: Student experiences of UK practice-based doctorates in art and design. *International Journal of Qualitative Studies in Education*, 18, 6, 713–728.

Colquhoun, J. (1977). The influence of social rank and fluoridation on dental treatment requirements. *New Zealand Dental Journal*, 73, 146–148.

Colquhoun, J. (1984). Disfiguring dental fluorosis in Auckland, New Zealand. *Fluoride* 17, 234–242.

Colquhoun, J. (1997). Why I changed my mind about water fluoridation. *Perspectives in Biology and Medicine*, 41, 1, 29–44.

Cooksey, D. (Chair). (2006). *A Review of UK Health Research Funding.* Norwich, UK: HMSO.

Corfield, P. (2007). The big picture's past, present and future. *The Times Higher Education Supplement,* July 27, 14.

Corlett, J.A. (2005). The good professor. *Journal of Academic Ethics,* 3, 27–54.

Cornwell, J. (2006). Slaves to American medicine, *The Sunday Times,* September 10.

Costley, C. & Gibbs, P. (2006). Researching others: Care as an ethic for practitioner researchers. *Studies in Higher Education,* 31, 1, 89–98.

Davidson, G., Garton, A.F. & Joyce, M. (2003). Survey of ethics education in Australian university schools and departments of psychology. *Australian Psychologist,* 38, 3, 216–222.

Davis, M. (2001). Students, academic institutions and contracts—a ticking time bomb? *Education and the Law,* 13, 1, 9–28.

De Vries, R., Anderson, M.S. & Martinson, B.C. (2006). Normal misbehavior: Scientists talk about the ethics of research. *Journal of Empirical Research on Human Research Ethics,* 1, 1, 43–50.

Delamont, S. (2005). Four great gates: Dilemmas, directions and distractions in educational research. *Research Papers in Education,* 20, 1, 85–100.

Deming, N., Fryer-Edwards, K. Dudzinski, D. Starks, H. Culver, J. Hopley, E. Robins, L. & Burke, W. (2007). Incorporating principles and practical wisdom in research ethics education: A preliminary study, *Academic Medicine,* 82, 1, 18–23.

Eagleton, T. (1996). *Literary theory: An introduction.* Oxford, UK: Blackwell.

Economic and Social Research Council (ESRC). (2006). *Research ethics framework,* http://www.esrcsocietytoday.ac.uk/esrcinfocentre/opportunities/research_ethics_framework/ (accessed on July 28, 2006).

Economic and Social Research Council (ESRC). (2007). *Annual Reports and Accounts, 2006–07.* London: The Stationery Office.

Eraut, M. (1994). *Developing professional knowledge and competence.* London: Falmer Press.

Ernst, E. (2001). Commentary: The Third Reich—German physicians between resistance and participation. *International Journal of Epidemiology,* 30, 1, 37–42.

Fengyan, W. (2004). Confucian thinking in traditional moral education: Key ideas and fundamental features. *Journal of Moral Education,* 33, 429–447.

Fetters, M. (1998). The family in medical decision-making: Japanese perspectives. *Journal of Clinical Ethics,* 9, 2, 132–146.

Finch, J. (1986). *Research and policy: The use of qualitative methods in social and educational research.* London: Falmer Press.

Finnis, J. (1994). Absolute human rights. In P. Singer, *Ethics* (Ed.), (pp. 256–258). Oxford, UK: Oxford University Press.

Fisher, C.B. & Kuther, T.L. (1997). Integrating research ethics into an introductory psychology course curriculum. *Teaching of Psychology,* 24, 3, 172–175.

Fjellstrom, R. (2005). Respect for persons, respect for integrity. *Medicine, Health Care and Philosophy*, 8, 231–242.

Foucault, M. (1972). *The archaeology of knowledge*, trans. A.M. Sherdian Smith. London: Tavistock Publications.

Franck, G. (1999). Scientific communication—A vanity fair?. *Science*, 286, 53–55.

Friedman, M. (1970). The social responsibility of business is to increase its profits. *The New York Times Magazine*, September 13.

Fuller, S. (2006). *The intellectual*. Cambridge, UK: Icon Books.

Gardiner, P. (2003). A virtue ethics approach to moral dilemmas in medicine. *Journal of Medical Ethics*, 29, 297–302.

Garfield, E. & Welljams-Dorof, A. (1992). Citation data: Their use as quantitative indicators for science and technology evaluation and policy-making. *Science and Public Policy*, 19, 5, 321–327.

Geary, N., Westlake, D. & Clarke, D. (1997). *Report to the researchers' lead body on the development of occupational standards for researchers*. London: Moloney & Geary.

Giddens, A. (1984). *The constitution of society*. London: Polity Press.

Gilligan, C., Ward, J.V. & Bardige, B. (1988). *Mapping the moral domain*. Cambridge, MA: Harvard University Press.

Gilson, E. (1929). *The philosophy of St. Thomas Aquinas*. Cambridge: W. Heffer & Sons Ltd.

Glover, J. (1977). *Causing death and saving lives*. Harmondsworth, UK: Penguin.

Goodlad, S. (1995). *The quest for quality: Sixteeen forms of heresy in higher education*. Buckingham, UK: The Society for Research into Higher Education/Open University Press.

Gordon, G. (2005). The human dimensions of the research agenda: Supporting the development of researchers throughout the career life cycle. *Higher Education Quarterly*, 59, 1, 40–55.

Grayson, J.P. & Myles, R. (2005). How research ethics boards are undermining survey research on Canadian university students. *Journal of Academic Ethics*, 2, 4, 293–314.

Greco, J. (2002). Virtues in epistemology. In P. Moser (Ed.), *Oxford Handbook of Epistemology* (pp. 287–315). New York: Oxford University Press.

Green, B. (2005). Unfinished business: Subjectivity and supervision. *Higher Education Research and Development*, 24, 2, 151–163.

Gregory, I. (2003). *Ethics in research*. London: Continuum.

Grinnell, F. (2002). The impact of ethics on research. *Chronicle of Higher Education* (The Chronicle Review Section 2), 4 October, B15.

Gutterman, L. (2006). Digging into the roots of research ethics. *Chronicle of Higher Education*, 9 January, 53, 2, 25.

Haggerty, K.D. (2004). Ethics creep: Governing social science research in the name of ethics. *Qualitative Sociology*, 27, 4, 391–414.

Halsey, A.H. & Trow, M.A. (1971). *The British academics*. London: Faber and Faber.

Hardwig, J. (1991). The role of trust in knowledge. *The Journal of Philosophy*, 88, 12, 693–708.

Harley, S. (2002). The impact of research selectivity on academic work and identity in UK universities. *Studies in Higher Education*, 27, 2, 187–205.

Harman, G. (2000). Allocating research infrastructure grants in post-binary higher education systems: British and Australian approaches. *Journal of Higher Education Policy and Management*, 22, 2, 111–126.

Harraway, D.J. (1988). Situated knowledges: The science question in feminism and the privilege of partial perspective. *Feminist Studies*, 14, 3, 575–597.

Hazlehurst, S. (2004). *A question of ethics: The changing management, governance and regulation of research in universities.* MA Dissertation, University of London: Institute of Education.

Healey, M. & Jenkins, A. (2005). *Institutional strategies to link teaching and research.* York, UK: Higher Education Academy.

HEFCE (Higher Education Funding Council for England). (2005). *PhD research degrees: Entry and completion,* Bristol, UK: HEFCE.

HEFCE (Higher Education Funding Council for England). (2007). *Research excellence framework: Consultation on the assessment and funding of higher education research post-2008.* Bristol, UK: HEFCE.

Henderson, M. & Salmon, A. (2005). Clone pioneer falls from grace, *The Times*, December 4, p. 3.

Hillier, Y. & Jameson, J. (2003). *Empowering researchers in further education,* Stoke-on-Trent, UK: Trentham Books.

Homan, R. (1991). *The ethics of social research.* London: Longman.

Honey, P. & Mumford, A. (1982). *The manual of learning styles,* Maidenhead, UK: Peter Honey.

Hood, J. (1998). Do corporations have social responsibilities?, *The Freeman*, 48, 11, November, http://www.fee.org/publications/the-freeman/article.asp?aid=3702, (accessed on February 10, 2008).

House of Commons Science and Technology Committee. (2007). *The Cooksey Report: Third Report of Session 2006–07.* London: The Stationery Office.

Hughes, J. (2005). Ethical cleansing? The process of gaining "ethical approval" for a new research project exploring performance in place of war. *Research in Drama Education*, 10, 2, 229–232.

Husserl, E. (1973). *The Idea of Phenomenology.* The Hague: Martin Nijhoff.

Hyland, K. (2001). Humble servants of the discipline?: Self-mention in research articles. *English for Specific Purposes*, 20, 207–226.

Jaffe, S. & Hyde, J. (2000). Gender differences in moral orientation: A meta-analysis, *Psychological Bulletin*, 126, 5, 703–726.

Jamrozik, K. (2004). Research ethics paperwork: What is the plot we seem to have lost?. *British Medical Journal*, 329, 286–287.

Janesick, V.J. (1994). The dance of qualitative research: metaphor, methodolatory and meaning. In N.K. Denzin and Y.S. Lincoln (Eds.), *A Handbook of Qualitative Research,* (pp. 209–219). London: Sage.

Jonsen, A.R. (1998). *The birth of bioethics.* Oxford, UK: Oxford University Press.

Judson, H.F. (2004). *The great betrayal: fraud in science.* Orlando, FL: Harcourt.

Kant, I. (1964). *Groundwork of the metaphysic of morals* (originally published in 1785), trans. H.J. Paton. London: Harper and Row.

Katz, J. (1972). *Experimentation with human subjects.* New York: Russell Sage.

Kennedy, B.D. (1997). *Academic duty.* Cambridge, MA: Harvard University Press.

Kiley, M. & Mullins, G. (2005). Supervisors' conceptions of research: What are they?. *Scandanavian Journal of Educational Research,* 49, 3, 245–262.

Kinser, K. (1998). Faculty at private for-profit universities: The university of Phoenix as a new model?. *International Higher Education,* 13, 13–14.

Kleinedler, S.R., Pickett, J.P. & Leonesio, C. (2005). *The Riverside dictionary of biography.* Boston and New York: Houghton Mifflin.

Knight, P.T. (2002). *Being a teacher in higher education.* Buckingham, UK: The Society for Research into Higher Education/Open University Press.

Kohlberg, L. (1984). Moral stages and moralization: The cognitive-developmental approach. In L. Kohlberg, (Ed.), *Essays on moral development: Volume 2. The psychology of moral development: The nature and validity of moral stages* (pp. 170–205). San Francisco, CA: Harper and Row.

Kolata, G. (1993). Scientist at work: Andrew Wiles; Math whiz who battled 350 year-old problem. *The New York Times,* 29 June.

Kolb, D.A. (1984). *Experiential learning experience as a source of learning and development.* New Jersey, NJ: Prentice Hall.

Koocher, G.P. & Keith-Spiegel, P.C. (1998). *Ethics in psychology: Professional standards and cases.* New York: Oxford University Press.

Kreber, C., Klampfleitner, M. McCune, V. Bayne, S. & Knottenbelt, M. (2007). What do you mean by "authentic"? A comparative review of the literature on conceptions of authenticity in teaching. *Adult Education Quarterly,* 58, 1, 22–43.

Kuhn, T. (1962). *The structure of scientific revolutions.* Chicago: University of Chicago Press.

Lather, P. (1986). Research as praxis. *Harvard Educational Review,* 56, 3, 257–277.

Lee, R.M. (1993). *Doing research on sensitive topics.* London: Sage.

Lee-Treweek, G. & Linkogle, S. (2000). *Danger in the field: Risk and ethics in social research.* London and New York: Routledge.

Leonard, D., Becker, R. & Coate, K. (2005). To prove myself at the highest level: The benefits of doctoral study. *Higher Education Research and Development,* 24, 2, 135–149.

Lingard, B. & Blackmore, J. (1997). The performative state and the state of educational research. *Australian Educational Researcher,* 24, 3, 1–30.

Louis, K.S., Holdsworth, J.M. Anderson, M.S. & Campbell, E.G. (2007). Becoming a scientist: The effects of group size and organizational climate. *Journal of Higher Education,* 78, 3, 311–336.

Louw, B. & Delport, R. (2006). Contextual challenges in South Africa: The role of a research ethics committee. *Journal of Academic Ethics*, 4, 39–60.

Lovitts, B.E. (2001). *Leaving the Ivory Tower: The causes and consequences of departure from doctoral study*. Lanham, MD: Rowan and Littlefield.

Lucas, C. (1996). *Crisis in the Academy*. London: Macmillan.

Lucas, L. (2006). *The research game in academic life*. Maidenhead: The Society for Research into Higher Education/Open University Press.

Luhmer, K., SJ (1990). Moral education in Japan. *Journal of Moral Education*, 19, 3, 172–181.

Macfarlane, B. (2004). *Teaching with integrity: The ethics of higher education practice*. London and New York: RoutledgeFalmer.

Macfarlane, B. (2007a). *The academic citizen: the virtue of service in university life*. Abingdon, UK: Routledge.

Macfarlane, B. (2007b). Beyond performance in teaching excellence. In A. Skelton (Ed.), *International perspectives on teaching excellence in higher education* (pp. 74–89). Abingdon, UK: Routledge.

Macfarlane, B. & Cheng, M. (2008). Communism, universalism and disinterestedness: Re- examining contemporary support among academics for Merton's scientific norms. *Journal of Academic Ethics*, 6, 1, 67–78.

Macfarlane, B. & Ottewill, R. (Eds.) (2001). *Effective learning and teaching in business and management*. London: Kogan Page.

MacIntyre, A. (1966). *A short history of ethics*. New York: Macmillan.

MacIntyre, A. (1981). *After virtue*. London: Duckworth.

Macklin, R. (1980). Problems in the teaching of ethics: Pluralism and indoctrination. In D. Callahan and S. Bok (Eds.), *Ethics teaching in higher education* (pp. 81–101). New York: Pelum Press.

Marr, A. (2004). *My trade: A short history of British journalism*. London: Macmillan.

Martin, E. & Booth, J. (2003). (Eds.) *Courageous research*. Altona, Australia: Common Ground Publishing.

Martinson, B. C., Anderson, M.S. & De Vries, R.G. (2005). Scientists behaving badly. *Nature*, 435, 737–738.

McNeil, P.M. (1993). *The ethics and politics of human experimentation*. Cambridge, UK: Cambridge University Press.

Medical Research Council. (2006). *Medical Research Council position statement on research regulation and ethics*, http://www.mrc.ac.uk/index/ publications_ethics_and_best_practice/publications (accessed on July 28, 2006).

Mendoza, P. (2007). Academic capitalism and doctoral student socialization: A case study, *Journal of Higher Education*, 78, 1, 71–96.

Merton, R. (1948). The self-fulfilling prophecy. *The Antioch Review*, 8, 193–210.

Merton, R. (1973a). Technical and moral dimensions of policy research (originally published in 1949). In N.W. Storer (Ed.), *The sociology of science:*

Theoretical and empirical investigations (pp. 70–98). Chicago: University of Chicago Press.

Merton, R. (1973b). Science and the social order (originally published in 1938). In N.W. Storer (Ed.), *The sociology of science: Theoretical and empirical investigations* (pp. 254–266). Chicago: University of Chicago Press.

Merton, R. (1973c). The normative structure of science (originally published in 1942). In N.W. Storer (Ed.), *The sociology of science: Theoretical and empirical investigations* (pp. 266–278). Chicago: University of Chicago Press.

Merton, R. (1973d). The Matthew Effect in science (originally published in 1968). In N.W. Storer (Ed.), *The sociology of science: Theoretical and empirical investigations* (pp. 439–459). Chicago: University of Chicago Press.

MEXT (The Ministry of Education, Culture, Sports, Science and Technology). (2006). *Basic principles concerning research misconduct*, available at http://www.scj.go.jp/en/kodo/index.html (accessed January 10, 2008).

Meyer, J.H.F. & Land, R. (2006). (eds.) *Overcoming barriers to student understanding: Threshold concepts and troublesome knowledge.* London: Routledge.

Meyer, J.H.F., Shanahan, M.P. & Laugksch, R.C. (2005). Students' conceptions of research. I: A qualitative and quantitative analysis, *Scandanavian Journal of Educational Research,* 49, 3, 225–244.

Mills, C.W. (1970). *The sociological imagination* (originally published in 1959). London: Pelican Books.

Mitscherlich, A. & Mielke, F. (1949). *Doctors of infamy.* New York: H. Schuman.

Moed, H.F. (2005). *Citation analysis in research evaluation.* Dordrecht: Springer.

Moed, H.F., Glänzel, W. & Schmoch, U. (Eds.) (2004). *Handbook of quantitative science and technology research: The use of publication and patent statistics in studies of S&T systems* (pp. 389–406). Dordrecht: Kluwer Academic Publishers.

Monbiot, G. (2006). *Heat: How to stop the planet burning.* London: Allen Lane.

Murtonen, M. (2005). University students' research orientations: Do negative attitudes exist toward quantitative methods?. *Scandanavian Journal of Educational Research,* 49, 3, 263–280.

Murtonen, M. & Lehtinen, E. (2003). Difficulties experienced by education and sociology students in quantitative methods courses. *Studies in Higher Education,* 28, 2, 171–185.

Murtonen, M. & Lehtinen, E. (2005). Conceptions of research and methodology learning. *Scandanavian Journal of Educational Research,* 49, 3, 217–224.

National Commission for the Protection of Human Subjects in Biomedical and Behavioral Research. (1979). *The Belmont Report: Ethical principles and guidelines for the protection of human subjects of research.* Washington, DC: U.S. Government Printing Office.

National Committee of Inquiry into Higher Education ("The Dearing Report"). (1997). *Higher Education in the Learning Society*. London: HMSO.

Neumann, R. (2007). Policy and practice in doctoral education. *Studies in Higher Education*, 32, 4, 459–473.

Nitterhouse, D. (2003). Plagiarism—not just an "academic" problem. *Teaching Business Ethics*, 7, 3, 215–227.

Nixon, J. (2004). Education for the good society: The integrity of academic practice. *London Review of Education*, 2, 3, 245–252.

Nixon, J. (2006). Relationships of virtue: Rethinking the goods of civil association. *Ethics and Education*, 1, 2, 149–161.

Noble, K.A. (1994). *Changing doctoral degrees: An international perspective*. Buckingham, UK: The Society for Research into Higher Education/Open University Press.

Olweny, C. (2007). The ethics and conduct of cross-cultural research in developing countries. *Psycho-Oncology*, 3, 1, 11–20.

O'Neil, O. (2002). *A question of trust*, Cambridge, UK: Cambridge University Press.

Palfreyman, D. (2007). £400k for educational malpractice by university academics. *Education and the Law*, 18, 2–3, 217–220.

Penslar, R.L. (Ed.) (1995). *Research ethics: cases and materials*, Bloomington and Indianapolis: Indiana University Press.

Petryna, A. (2002). *Life exposed: Biological citizens after Chernobyl*. Princeton, NJ: Princeton University Press.

Pimple, K.D. (1995). General issues in teaching research ethics. In R.L. Penslar (Ed.), *Research Ethics: Cases and Materials* (pp. 3–12). Bloomington and Indianapolis: Indiana University Press.

Pincoffs, E. (1986). *Quandaries and virtues: Against reductivism in ethics*, Lawrence: University Press of Kansas.

Platt, J. (1981). On interviewing one's peers. *British Journal of Sociology*, 32, 1, 75–91.

Polanyi, M. (1967). *The tacit dimension*. New York: Anchor Books.

Powell, T. (2006). Cultural context in medical ethics: Lessons from Japan. *Philosophy, Ethics, and Humanities in Medicine*, 1, 4, http://www.peh-med.com/content/1/1/4.

Power, M. (1997). *The audit society: Rituals of verification*, Oxford, UK: Oxford University Press.

Powers, D.A. & Ellison, C.G. (1995). Interracial contact and Black racial attitudes: The contact hypothesis and selectivity bias. *Social Forces*, 74, 1, 205–226.

Pring, R. (2001). The virtues and vices of an educational researcher. *Journal of Philosophy of Education*, 35, 3, 407–421.

Prospect. (2006). *Prospect science survey*. London: Prospect.

Quality Assurance Agency for Higher Education (QAA). (2004). *Code of practice for the assurance of academic quality and standards in higher education, Section 1: Postgraduate research programmes*. Gloucester, UK: QAA.

Rachels, J. (1999). *The elements of moral philosophy*. London: McGraw-Hill.

Rawls, J. (1971). *A theory of justice*, Cambridge, MA: Harvard University Press.

Respect. (2006). *The RESPECT Code of Practice*, http://www.respectproject.org/code/index.php (accessed on May 31, 2006).

Reverby, S.M. (Ed.) (2000). *Tuskegee's truths: Rethinking the Tuskegee syphilis study*. Chapel Hill: University of North Carolina Press.

Robertson, J. & Blackler, G. (2006). Students' experiences of learning in a research environment. *Higher Education Research and Development*, 25, 3, 215–229.

Rosenthal, R. & Jacobson, L. (1968). *Pygmalion in the classroom*. New York: Rinehart and Winston.

Rosnow, R.L. (1990). Teaching research ethics through role-play and discussion. *Teaching of Psychology*, 17, 3, 179–181.

Rout, M. & Knott, M. (2007). Canberra dumps much-maligned RQF. *The Australian* (Higher Education section), December 21.

Rovner, S.L. (2007). Research ethics: Experts ponder how best to prevent and respond to scientific misconduct as three Japanese cases conclude. *Chemistry and Engineering News*, February 12, 85, 7, 76–79.

Rugg, G. & Petre, M. (2004). *The unwritten rules of PhD research*. Maidenhead, UK: Open University Press.

Ryle, G. (1972). Can virtue be taught?. In R. F. Dearden, P. H. Hirst & R. S. Peters (Eds.), *Education and Development of Reason* (pp. 434–447). London: Routledge and Kegan Paul.

Salmon, P. (1994). Research students' perspectives. In S. Haselgrove (Ed.), *The Student Experience* (pp. 141–145). Buckingham, UK: The Society for Research into Higher Education/Open University Press.

Sayers, D.L. (2003). *Gaudy night* (originally published in 1935). London: Hodder and Stoughton.

Schwehn, M.R. (1993). *Exiles From Eden: Religion and the academic vocation in America*, Oxford, UK: Oxford University Press.

Science Council of Japan (SCJ). (2006). *Code of conduct for scientists*, available at http://www.scj.go.jp/en/kodo/index.html (accessed January 8, 2008).

Scott, D., Brown, A., Lunt, I., Thorne, L. (2004). *Professional doctorates: Integrating professional and academic knowledge*. Maidenhead, UK: Open University Press.

Senior, K. & Hay, T. (2005). Is it "writing" or "writing up"? Authenticity, voice and the educational researcher. Paper presented at the British Educational Research Association Annual Conference, University of Glamorgan, September 14–17.

Shils, E. (Ed. and trans.) (1973). *Max Weber on universities: The power of the state and the dignity of the academic calling in Imperial Germany*. Chicago: University of Chicago Press.

Shils, E. (1997). *The calling of education: The academic ethic and other essays on higher education*. Chicago: University of Chicago Press.

Siegelman, S.S. (1991). Assassins and zealots: Variations in peer review. *Radiology*, 178, 3, 636–642.

Skelton, A. (2005). *Understanding teaching excellence in higher education: Towards a critical approach.* London: Routledge.

Smiles, S. (1910). *Character.* London: John Murray.

Smith, D. (1999). The changing idea of a university. In D. Smith and A.K. Langslow (Eds.), *The idea of a university* (pp. 148–174). London: Jessica Kingsley.

Smith, R. (2006). Commentary: The power of the unrelenting impact factor— Is it a force for good or harm?. *International Journal of Epidemiology*, 35, 1129–1130.

Smith, R. (2008). Beware the tyranny of impact factors. *Journal of Bone and Joint Surgery*, 90, 2, 125–126.

Stedman, Y., Yamamura, J.H. & Beekun, R.I. (2007). Gender differences in business ethics: Justice and relativist perspectives. *Business Ethics: A European Review*, 16, 2, 163–174.

Stierer, B. (2007). HE lecturers researching HE issues: A problematic element of contemporary academic practice. Paper presented at the Annual Conference of the Society for Research into Higher Education: Reshaping Higher Education, December 11–13, 2007, Brighton, UK.

Stelfox, H., Chua, G., O'Rourke, K., & Detsky, A.S. (1998). Conflict of interest in the debate over calcium-channel anatogonists. *New England Journal of Medicine*, 338, 2, 101–106.

Straker, A. & Hall, E. (1999). From clarity to chaos and back: Some reflections on the research process. *Educational Action Research*, 7, 3, 419–432.

Strand, D. (1998). *Research in the creative arts,* Canberra, Australia: Department of Employment, Education, Training and Youth Affairs.

Strohmetz, D.B. & Skleder, A.A. (1992). The use of role-play in teaching research ethics: A validation study. *Teaching of Psychology*, 19, 2, 106–108.

Swazey, J.P. & Bird, S.J. (1997). Teaching and learning research ethics. In D. Elliott, and J.E. Stern (Eds.), *Research ethics: A reader* (pp. 1–19). Hanover, USA: University of New England.

Talib, A. & Steele, A. (2000). The Research Assessment Exercise: Strategies and trade-offs. *Higher Education Quarterly*, 54, 1, 68–87.

Taylor, C. (1991). *The ethics of authenticity.* Cambridge, MA: Harvard University Press.

Thomas, H.G. (2001). Funding mechanism or quality assessment: Responses to the Research Assessment Exercise in English institutions. *Journal of Higher Education Policy and Management*, 23, 171–179.

Thompson, P., Constantineau, P. & Fallis, G. (2005). Academic citizenship: An academic colleagues' working paper. *Journal of Academic Ethics*, 3, 2–4, 127–142.

Thorpe, R. & Moscarola, J. (1991). Detecting your research strategy. *Management Education and Development*, 22, 2, 127–133.

Tight, M. (2005). Higher education research as tribe, territory and/or community: A co-citation analysis. Annual Conference of the Society for Research into Higher Education: New Perspectives on Research into Higher Education, December 13–15, University of Edinburgh.

Tolhurst, D. (2007). The influence of learning environments on students' epistemological beliefs and learning outcomes. *Teaching in Higher Education,* 12, 2, 219–233.

Tooley, J. with D. Darby (1998). *Educational research: A critique. A survey of published research.* Office for Standards in London: Education.

University of the Arts. (2007). *Code of Practice on Research Ethics,* http://www.arts.ac.uk/ docs/Code_of_Practice_on_ Research_Ethics_pdf (accessed on October 28, 2007)

University of Greenwich. (2007). *University of Greenwich Research Ethics Policy 2007,* http://www.gre.ac.uk/research/research_ethics_committee/ policy (accessed on January 16, 2008)

Van Hooft, S. (2006). *Understanding virtue ethics.* Chesham: Acumen.

Vermunt, J.D. (2005). Conceptions of research and methodology learning, a commentary on the special issue. *Scandanavian Journal of Educational Research,* 49, 3, 329–334.

Von Humboldt, W. (1970). On the spirit and the organizational framework of intellectual institutions in Berlin. *Minerva,* 8, 242–250.

Walker, M. (2007). Goodbye blue skies?. *The Times Higher Education Supplement,* August 10.

Walkerdine, V. (2003). The search for self and spirit in suicidology. In E. Martin and J. Booth (Eds.), *Courageous Research* (pp. 129–139). Altona, Australia: Common Ground Publishing.

Warren, C.A.B. (1988). *Gender issues in field research.* Newbury Park, CA: Sage.

Webb, D. (2003). The search for self and spirit in suicidology. In E. Martin and J. Booth (Eds.), *Courageous Research* (pp. 25–44). Altona, Australia: Common Ground Publishing

Weber, C.E. (1995). *Stories of virtue in business.* Lanham, MD: University Press of America.

Weber, M. (1973a) The academic freedom of the universities (originally published in 1909). In E. Shils (Ed.), and trans. *Max Weber On Universities: The power of the state and the dignity of the academic calling in Imperial Germany,* (pp. 18–23). Chicago: University of Chicago Press.

Weber, M. (1973b) Science as a vocation (originally published in 1919). In E. Shils (Ed.), and trans. *Max Weber On Universities: The power of the state and the dignity of the academic calling in Imperial Germany,* (pp. 54–62). Chicago: The University of Chicago Press.

Williams, B. (1994). Jim and the Indians. In P. Singer (Ed.), *Ethics* (pp. 339–345). Oxford: Oxford University Press.

Williams, B. (2002). *Truth and truthfulness: An essay in genealogy.* Princeton and Oxford, UK: Princeton University Press.

Williams, S. & Robinson, G. (2007). *Research and policy: An INCORE consultative review of research processes, research priorities and the usefulness of research to policy-makers at the United Nations and other international agencies,* http://www.incore.ulst.ac.uk/publications/needs.pdf (accessed on April 19, 2007)

Willig, C. (2001). *Introducing qualitative research in psychology: Adventures in theory and method,* Buckingham, UK: Open University Press.

Wisker, G., Robinson, G., Trafford, V., Creighton, E. & Warnes, M. (2003). Recognizing and overcoming dissonance in postgraduate student research. *Studies in Higher Education,* 28, 1, 91–105.

Yorke, M. (1999). Editorial. *Studies in Higher Education,* 24, 1, 5–6.

Zhang, L., Lopez, P., He, T., Yu, W. & Ho, D.D. (2004). Retraction of an interpretation (Letter), *Science,* 303, 5657, 417–572.

Zhang, Y. & Moore, K.E. (2005). A class demonstration using deception to promote student involvement with research ethics. *College Teaching,* 53, 4, 155–157.

INDEX